DIVINE CHARACTER

Westminster Profiles and Spirituality

David W. Hall

The Covenant Foundation

© 2019

Cover graphics: Westminster Abbey by Thomas H. Shepherd, Wikipedia Commons: https://commons.wikimedia.org/w/index.php?title=File:Westminster_Abbey_Thomas_Hosmer_Shepherd.png&oldid=111221089

© 2019
The Covenant Foundation
648 Goldenwood Court
Powder Springs, GA 30127
(david.hall@midwaypca.org)

All Rights reserved. No part of this publication may be reproduced or transmitted in any form or by any means, electronic or mechanical, without written permission from the publisher, except for inclusion in a magazine, newspaper or broadcast.

Hall, David W.
Divine Character

1. Westminster Assembly;   2. Church History;
3. Reformed Theology;   4. Spirituality;

First Edition 2019

TABLE OF CONTENTS

Preface	1
Thomas Gataker	3
William Gouge	6
Simeon Ashe	9
Jeremiah Burroughs	13
Edmund Calamy	15
Thomas Case	17
John Dury	20
Stephen Marshall	22
Herbert Palmer	25
Lazarus Seaman	28
Anthony Tuckney	30
Richard Vines	32
Samuel Rutherford	34
William Twisse	36
Lord Warriston	39
George Gillespie	42
Alexander Henderson	45
Westminster Spirituality: A Commemorative Essay	51
Bibliography	89

Preface and Dedication

These brief profiles were originally prepared in 1992-1993 as part of the 350th commemoration of the Westminster Assembly. After many years, most of us will find that their enduring value still inspires us today. Surely, their spirituality exceeds that of average pastors and theologians; thus, we should set ourselves to learning from them.

These pastor-theologians were supported by Parliament and their congregations. I am happy to acknowledge my debt to the two fine congregations that have supported our ministry for 36 years: Covenant Presbyterian (PCA) in Oak Ridge, TN, where these were originally researched; and Midway Presbyterian (PCA) in Powder Springs, GA, where these are being presented this year.

Thank you for your prayers, support, and fellowship of ordinary means of grace pastoral ministry and scholarship.

Thomas Gataker

Thomas Gataker (1574-1654) lived a full life of eighty years, having received the first principles of the faith from his father, who was a pastor in London. At an early age Gataker took a healthy delight in books and had the advantages of a good education, possessing a vigorous mind, which absorbed the principles of the faith quickly. In addition, he was a superb student in the Greek language, even continuing his morning devotions in the original languages throughout his life.

As early as 1596 he was appointed as a fellow at Sidney College even before the buildings were completed. And while he was widely drawn upon as an academic, he resisted serving as a minister because he had such exalted respect for the office. Many of his students from Sidney College went on to illustrious careers, while Mr. Gataker preached on the Lord's Day at Everton during his tenure on the faculty. In 1603 he received his Divinity degree at Cambridge, but while pursuing his doctorate, he was forced to cease his studies for reasons of economics.

Although Gataker was quickly establishing a reputation as an excellent scholar, following his marriage in 1611 he accepted the rectorship at Rotherhithe in Surrey near London. Along with ministering on the Lord's Day, he also established a Friday Catechism lecture which was chiefly designed for the instruction of young children. Gataker saw great value in the instruction of youth.

In 1624 Gataker authored one of the earliest reformed Catechisms in England, "A Short Catechism," along with *A Discussion of the Popish Doctrine of Transubstantiation*. Moreover, he became an expert on the theological topic of justification, bringing his expertise to influence the thought of the Westminster teaching on the doctrine of justification.

While sitting with the Westminster Assembly during the 1640s, he was offered the Chancellorship of Trinity College in Cambridge by the Earl of Manchester but declined. In his association with other Westminster Assembly divines, he helped develop a commentary on biblical texts, entitled *English Annotations,* contributing the commentaries on Isaiah, Jeremiah and Lamentations. In the late 1640s he returned to his first love, authoring an excellent textbook on the style of the New Testament, and in the 1650s he composed several works on classical Greek and Roman authors.

Although Gataker was certainly one of the most respected thinkers of his time, he also was a very practical man. After the conclusion of the Westminster Assembly, when he had retired from the ministry, it was his practice to open up his home to a time of catechetical instruction for his children and other young English gentlemen or foreigners staying in his home. Under this tutelage many people were built up in the faith and he also showed his concern for his own children. In addition, Gataker was a generous man, giving his alms in secret. In his last Will he left 50 pounds to the poor of his parish, 50 pounds to ten ministers who were in poor financial condition, and 5 pounds each to eight ministers' widows.

Simeon Ashe records Gataker's dying words: "I am now conflicting with my last adversary, though I believe the sting is taken out. Nature will struggle, but I humbly submit unto the good pleasure of God. I heartily beg the pardon of my many sins, especially of my want of ... fidelity in my public and private charge, hoping to be washed with Christ's blood, and desiring to be translated out of this restless condition. I expect daily, yea hourly to be translated into that everlasting rest, which God hath prepared for them who are interested in his Christ. And I pray God to bless you, and his whole ministry every where."

Having been forty-three years pastor at Rotherhithe, his funeral sermon was preached from Proverbs 16:31, by his much esteemed friend, Mr. Simeon Ashe.

Gataker thus gives us a lasting example of the pious blend of scholarship and holiness, and his name is remembered for excellence as a scholar, ranked with Selden and Ussher. Amidst all the recognition of his intellect and ability, he was also an excellent pastor, a loving father and diaconal giver, a worthy model to imitate: "Fathers do not exasperate your children, but raise them up in the nurture and discipline of the Lord" (Eph. 6:4).

William Gouge

William Gouge (1575-1653) was born in Middlesex County, England and was incredibly attentive to secret prayer and the sanctifying of the Lord's Day from a young age. He entered King's College in Cambridge in 1595 and during his nine years at Cambridge was known for his attendance at morning prayers which usually began at 5:30 a.m. Gouge also resolved to read 15 chapters a day from the Holy Scriptures, taking up five in the morning, five after dinner, and five before he went to bed. This knowledge of Scripture permeated his life, writing, and ministry.

While at Cambridge, a Jewish Rabbi took residence to teach the Hebrew language, and Gouge became one of his best students. Following his graduation he was not only an excellent Hebrew scholar, but also a lecturer in logic and philosophy in the college. In the year 1607 he was ordained to the ministry and commenced his ministry at Black Friars Church (London) in the following year. He often said that the pinnacle of his ambition was to go from Black Friars directly to heaven, and as Mr. Gouge discharged his duty in the pastoral office with exemplary diligence and faithfulness, his wish was apparently granted having served his entire ordained ministry of 46 years as minister at Black Friars. He is an excellent example to us of the value of lengthy tenure in the pastoral ministry to a church.

Although he was very well educated, his manner of preaching was clear to the common man. His style was familiar as he taught, for example: "Remember, we do not mount the pulpit to say fine things, or eloquent things, we have there to proclaim the good tidings of salvation to fallen men; to point out the way of eternal life; to exhort, to cheer and support the suffering sinner; these are the glorious topics upon which we have to enlarge—and will these permit the tricks of oratory, or the studied beauties of eloquence? Shall truths and counsels like these be couched in terms which the poor and ignorant cannot comprehend? Let all eloquent preachers beware lest they fill any man's ear with sounding words, when they should be feeding his soul with the bread of everlasting life!—Let them fear lest instead of honoring God, they honor themselves! If any man ascend the pulpit with the intention of uttering "A Fine Thing," he is committing a deadly sin."

Following his exposition at the worship service, neighbors who were unable to attend came to his own house where he repeated his sermons to them in a common manner, as one means of lengthening his concern for the unchurched. Having a particular sensitivity to the Sabbath from early on, Gouge carried that commitment throughout his life. His own house servants were not required to provide Saturday evening meals so that they might go to bed and prepare for the Lord's day. Says Gouge about the value of the Sabbath as an indicator of spiritual vitality, "Men, by the manner in which they 'regard this day to the Lord,' discover the real complexion of their minds relative to him. This day will declare whether they have any knowledge and fear of God, any faith, hope, and delight in him, any love to, or desire after him." So steadfast was his adherence to the Sabbath that opponents mocked Gouge by calling him the Archpuritan.

He received his Bachelor of Divinity degree (1611) and his doctorate from Cambridge (1628). While serving in the Westminster Assembly he was frequently called on to be moderator *pro tem* in the absence of the moderator, and early in October of 1644 Gouge was one of the leaders appointed to the committee to examine prospective ministers. He also was the author of the *English Annotations* (the Bible Commentary by the Westminster Divines) on First Kings through the Book of Job. Later he was chosen as President of Sion College which was a hot bed of puritanism. Gouge also exemplified the generosity of true piety when he supported poor scholars in the university at his own expense, as well as liberally giving to others who were impoverished. He was a bright example of benevolence.

Dr. Gouge routinely rose about 4:00 a.m. to have his own morning devotions, and often engaged in solemn and extraordinary exercises of prayer and fasting, encouraging many a Christian by his own private fasting. Of his desire to love Christ with all his soul, mind and strength, his words have been recorded: "When I look upon myself, I see nothing but emptiness and weakness; but when I look upon Christ, I see nothing but fulness and sufficiency. Everything that we need is found in Christ, and may be derived from him as the vital head of the Church. . . . One thing we are certain of—that no being in the universe can fill his place, and do for us what he is able to do."

In his dying it was evident that he had a great piety. To his friends who came to visit him in his sickness he said, "I am willing to die, having, I bless God, nothing to do but to die." He called death his best friend next to Jesus Christ. Upon his death he was greatly missed in the Black Friars pulpit, having lived through a tumultuous age and dying shortly after the culmination of the Westminster Assembly, providentially before the Great Ejection of 1662, when most puritan leaders were forced out of their pulpits. His spiritual legacy was passed on by one of his assistants (William Jenkin), his minister son Thomas Gouge, and his son-in-law Richard Roberts who married his eldest daughter, all three of which excellent divines took their stand with Christ and together were ejected in 1662. Gouge could well say, "As for me and my house, we will serve the Lord" (Josh. 24:15).

Simeon Ashe

Simeon Ashe was educated at Emmanuel College at Cambridge in the early seventeenth century and began his preaching ministry in Staffordshire, England, an affluent neighborhood with many eminent citizens. Later he was chaplain to the Earl of Manchester, also serving faithfully as a chaplain in the Army in 1642, along with a number of other men who would later become divines of the Westminster Assembly. Ashe served as minister at Michael Basing-Shaw in London, and later at St. Austin's in London until his death.

Throughout his ministry Simeon Ashe opposed hierarchical and Episcopal practices, and when criticized for such principled opposition, quickly pled guilty. Ashe was distinguished by academic prowess and the ardor and zeal of his ministry. He was one of the signers of an early pro-puritan tract entitled, *A Vindication of the Ministers of the Gospel in, and about London, from the Unjust Aspersions cast upon their former actings for the Parliament, as if they had promoted the King's death.*

According to James Reid, "Mr. Ashe had a good estate, and a liberal heart. He was very hospitable; and his house was much frequented, and he himself was highly esteemed. He was a Christian of the primitive simplicity; and a non-conformist of the old stamp. He was eminently distinguished, by a holy life, and a cheerful mind. Holiness is the bright ornament of the Christian, the glory of angels, the beauty of heaven, and the express image of God himself, who is glorious in holiness. And persons who are most strict and holy in their lives ought to be most esteemed and honored. But such persons are too often hated, reproached, and persecuted, by the world lying in wickedness, who scoff at holiness, and thereby deride God himself. Holiness is peculiarly becoming, in the ministers of religion, who *minister about holy things*, and ought to be exemplary to the people, in their lives."

At his funeral he was eulogized by Edmund Calamy, and much of his character is revealed in the words of his fellow Westminster divine. Calamy said that Ashe was, "A man of great sincerity, humility, benevolence, prudence, and patience: as eminently diligent in preaching the glorious gospel of the grace of God in season and out of season, so as not to please the ear, but to wound the heart; seeking not the applause of men, but the salvation of souls: as singularly careful in visiting the sick: as excelling in prayer, and in maintaining great acquaintance and communion with God. His death was conformable to his life. He was rich in faith, and in other fruits of the Holy Spirit, and an eminent follower of those who through faith and *patience* inherit the promises. He died very comfortably, in the cheerful exercise of faith, and abounding in the consolations of the gospel of Christ, molested neither with doubts nor fears. His conversation was deeply interesting, and very edifying. Like the torch, he illuminated all around him, he did eminently bear witness to the truth and the power of the Christian religion, at this trying season. And he was peculiarly attentive to the spiritual improvement of those who were about him. He warmly recommended Jesus Christ to them."

Mr. Calamy says, "When I was with him he took occasion to complain much, and not without just cause, that ministers, when they met together, discoursed not more of Christ, of heaven, and of the concernments of the other world; professing that if God should restore him, he would be more careful in his discourses, and more fruitful than ever he had been. He exhorted me and other ministers to preach much of Jesus Christ, and to speak of Christ to him; saying, When I consider my best duties, I sink, I die, I despair; but when I think of Christ, I have enough; he is all and in all. I desire to know nothing but Jesus Christ and him crucified. I account all things dung and dross, that I may be found in Christ."

Upon his death it was said that the church had lost a choice pillar and that the city of London had lost an ancient, faithful minister. He was called a "Bezaleel in God's tabernacle, a master builder, an old disciple—a burning and shining light." Samuel Rutherford spoke of him as the "Gracious and zealous Mr. Ashe." Says one biographer, "Mr. Ashe, desiring to know nothing but Jesus Christ and him crucified, in this awful season, said farther: 'It is one thing to speak of Christ and of heaven, and another thing to feel the consolation of Christ and of heaven, as I do:' when he clapped his hand upon his breast, rejoicing with joy unspeakable and full of glory. . . . At another time, he said, 'The comforts of a holy life are real, and soul-supporting. I feel the reality of them, and you may know by me, that it is not in vain to serve God.' His religious exercises, and his lively edifying conversation, were highly acceptable to those who visited him in his sickness; and they may be highly useful to posterity. He closed an active and holy life, by a pious and edifying death, on the 20th of August 1662, a short time before the fatal Bartholomew-day commemoration. His mortal remains were buried on the 23d of August in the church of St. Austin."

One historian has gathered together a few choice sayings of Mr. Ashe, among which are: "'*Without me*, saith Christ, *you can do nothing*; neither without him can we endure any thing. And he only can support the sinking soul under the most smarting troubles and heavy oppressions.--We may safely sail through Christ's blood into the bosom of the Father.--Truth, not words, feeds the soul: and I much rather desire, in my ministry, to profit, than to please, my auditory.--Former failings bewailed, shall not interrupt the course of future kindness."

He frequently preached before Mayors, Sheriffs, Aldermen, and commanders of military forces as a chaplain. One of his well known sermons was "God's Incomparable Goodness Unto Israel, Unfolded and Applied," preached before the House of Commons toward the end of the Westminster Assembly on April 28, 1647. Moreover Ashe is known as a eulogist of sorts himself, giving the funeral orations for other Westminster divines such as Jeremiah Whitaker,

Ralph Robinson, Robert Strange, Thomas Gataker, and Richard Vines. He wrote *The Power of Godliness* and co-authored *A Treatise on the Covenant of Grace.*

Jeremiah Burroughs

Jeremiah Burroughs (1599-1646) was one of the other leaders of the Westminster Assembly who was also educated at Cambridge. Early on in his ministry, despite the persecution under Bishop Wren and Archbishop Laud, Burroughs consistently protested against the state-church, even temporarily undergoing self-exile, relocating to Holland where he became minister of an English congregation in Rotterdam. There he continued for some time, but upon returning to England he served as pastor in two of the largest congregations in the city of London. He was an independent who maintained candor, modesty, and charity.

As far as his preaching, "he did not use 'those gaudy ornaments which too often put the preacher in the place of his text; or, as one has well expressed it, serve only to evaporate weighty truths, and to make them appear as light as the style.'—His great aim was to guide his hearers in the way to heaven; and accordingly, plainness and persuasion were the chief objects of his attention. The plain Calvinistic doctrine of the Reformation was honored with wonderful success, in promoting the interests of the Redeemer's kingdom, at that time."

Jeremiah Burroughs was an "esteemed and great ornament of the pulpit" and was known as the morning star of Stepney, the large congregation he pastored. Burroughs was also a writer of great penetration, handling extensive and difficult subjects with uncommon evangelical piety. Cotton Mather, patriarch of American Christianity, gave great praise for Burroughs, who died at a fairly young age, 47, on November 14, 1646. He was known as an excellent scholar, a good expositor, and a popular preacher.

Burroughs has a lasting witness through many of his writings. Not only was he known for his practical commentary on *Hosea* (four volumes!), but also for numerous sermons preached at public thanksgivings and before the House of Peers and the House of Lords in the 1640s. He was also the author of a devotional guide totaling 754 pages on Hebrews 11:25-26, *Moses's Choice, with his eye fixed upon Heaven: discovering the happy condition of a self-denying heart*. Divisions among Independents and Presbyterians so greatly grieved his heart, that in later life he wrote a plea for unity among Christians, *Irenicum, to the Lovers of Truth and Peace: Heart-divisions opened, and the causes and evils of them: With cautions that we may not be hurt by them, and endeavors to heal them*. Among his other works were *Gospel Worship: The Right Manner of Sanctifying the Name of God in General* (published posthumously in 1648), *Gospel Conversation* (also published posthumously), a series of sermons which explain how we walk, and *The Gospel, Two Treatises*, one of which was on "Earthly Mindedness" with the second treatise on the "Exceeding Sinfulness of Sin." Perhaps Burroughs is most widely known for his *The Saints' Treasury* or his sermons on the Beatitudes, *The Saints' Happiness* (both recently reprinted). Burroughs is an enduring example of the union of godly learning with depth of piety.

Edmund Calamy

Edmund Calamy (1600-1666) was one of the most learned of the Westminster Assembly divines. He graduated with his Bachelor of Divinity from Cambridge in 1632 and early on in his life took a disliking to Arminianism. Of his studious personality it was said that he studied 16 hours a day, particularly mastering the medieval scholastics, and was rumored to have read Augustine's works five times.

Still, however, when he preached he was concerned with plain and vernacular terms, much preferring the reading of Holy Scriptures to any other works. Mr. Calamy was chosen to serve as a lecturer at Bury in Suffolk County while laboring alongside of Jeremiah Burroughs. In 1639 he became the Minister of Mary Aldermanbury in London and in 1640 joined with five men (who would eventually become members of the Westminster Assembly) to author a famous tract attacking the liturgy and episcopacy of the Anglican Church as being incongruous with biblical presbyterianism. This book was published with the author identified as "Smectymnuus", an acronym for the first letters of the following men's names: Stephen Marshall, Edmund Calamy, Thomas Young, Mathew Newcomen, and William Spurstow. In this 1641 tract, which in many ways struck the match that would lead to the Westminster Assembly, the treatise discussed the parity of bishops and presbyters in scripture, as well as the ancient institution of ruling elders in the church. It also pointed out that the Episcopal form of government was a serious departure from biblical rule.

Through this and many other works Calamy gained a shining reputation in London, where he was "eminently distinguished by his intrepid integrity, ministerial faithfulness, solid learning, and genuine piety. He made vigorous efforts, for the progress of useful knowledge among mankind, in overthrowing error, and in defending and propagating truth." When many Irish Protestants received difficult treatment at the hands of the Roman Catholic Church, Calamy's church took up a very liberal collection to assist them, thus continuing the apostolic practice of being concerned for those in distress (Gal. 2:10).

Mr. Calamy was an eager advocate for the divine institution of the ruling elder, and he was among the first to openly defend before Parliament that bishop and presbyter were one. He was also one of the more popular preachers in London and a frequent preacher before the Long Parliament. Toward the end of his ministry, Calamy was removed from his pulpit at Aldermanbury by the 1662 Act of Uniformity, which required obedience to state-imposed forms and unbiblical rituals.

Even though offered a position as a bishop, Calamy, like Moses rejected the riches of this world, refusing to enjoy the pleasures of sin for a season, valuing rather the things of the Lord. Later in life Calamy was imprisoned in Newgate and was criticized for not conforming to the wishes of the King and Bishop, at last dying in October of 1666.

Calamy has left behind a long written record. Much of Calamy's thought is preserved in his 1654 *Jus Divinum* (on church government), a number of his sermons, and the posthumous *Treatise of Meditation*. Perhaps one of his greatest legacies was his eldest son, who also was one of the ministers ejected by the Act of Uniformity. His grandson was also a dissenting (a non-conformist to that state-imposed religion) divine of great eminence who left behind other learned works. Calamy was a shining example of the faith which, rejecting this world's favors, regards disgrace for the sake of Christ as of greater value than the treasures of Egypt (Heb. 11:25).

Thomas Case

Thomas Case was the son of a minister in the County of Kent in England. He was trained up as a child, and the training paid off: "'The importance of early instruction is written upon the whole system of nature, and repeated in every page of the history of Providence. You may bend a young twig and make it receive almost any form; but that which has attained to maturity, and taken its ply, you will never bring into another shape than that which it naturally bears.'--Children may undoubtedly receive much benefit by the use of means, in a very early period of life. And when parents use the means, they ought carefully to remember the beautiful connection between the duty and the promise." As a youthful convert, he quickly learned that prayer is one of the mainstays of the Christian life, the very breath of regenerate persons. In 1616 he became a student at Oxford where he graduated with his Masters in 1623. He was first chosen a lecturer and then later pastor of Mary Magdalen Church in Milk Street in London.

Thomas Case was a pioneer for morning prayer exercises. Case solicited prayer requests for the various needs in the city, indeed being an example of a city-wide prayer ministry. Case and a number of other ministers agreed to separate a half hour early in the morning to be spent in prayer, with another half given to an exhortation. Mr. Case began his morning exercises at 7:00 a.m. and great fruit blossomed from these prayer ministries.

Case was frequently called upon to preach to the Parliament on public occasions. In preparation for adopting the Solemn League and Covenant (1643), he preached several sermons to his congregation in the Milk Street Church, admonishing, "To every soul that shall enter into this holy league and covenant; my request is, that they would look around them: life and death is before them; if we break with God now, we have just cause to fear, God will stand to covenant no more with us, but will avenge the quarrel, with our utter destruction; if we be sincere and faithful, this covenant will be a foundation of much peace, joy, glory, and security, to us, and our seed, to the coming of Christ, which that it may be, shall be the earnest prayer of him, who is thy servant for Jesus' sake."

Case, as Edmund Calamy had been, was a preacher at Aldermanbury and then later was pastor of one of the largest churches, Giles' Cripplegate. Even though he was an outstanding pastor in this flagship church, his opposition to Archbishop Laud managed to have him confined to prison for six months for not submitting to him. Following the Westminster Assembly, Case was a representative at the Savoy Conference (1661), and in 1662 he was silenced with his brothers by the Act of Uniformity or the Great Ejection. He died at the ripe old age of 84 in 1682 on the 30th of May, which ranked Mr. Case among the longest living of those who composed the Westminster Confession. In doctrine he was a strict Calvinist and his writings included the following: *Correction, Instruction: or, A Treatise of Afflictions* (1653), *Imitation of the Saints opened in Practical Meditations* (1666), and *Mount Pisgah: or, A Prospect of Heaven* (1670).

In his farewell sermon, Case lamented the state of spirituality in England at the time as follows: "In things of the world we are all in all, and all in every part; . . . but in prayer, how many things are we doing?" He also decried the absence of concern for Christians in other places. Case preached: "When did we go to bed sick for the afflictions of God's people abroad? When did their miseries cost us an hour's sleep? or a meal's meat? When did we lie in the dust, and cry out, Ah Lord! their glory! Because we have not shed tears for their blood, God may justly say, 'The next turn of persecution shall be yours.'" Case advocated a faith which was concerned for other Christians outside of his own nation. One of the secrets of Case's ministry was that early in the morning, he along with other Godly servants met with the Lord. We could use more of that today. "Early in the morning our song will rise to Thee."

John Dury

John Dury was born at the beginning of the seventeenth century in Scotland and began his studies at Oxford in 1624. He was fluent in German and became conversant with several other language groups within the reformed family. John Dury's life-long passion was to promote reconciliation, first between Calvinist and Lutherans, and then among other groups throughout the Christian world. He was characterized by an exceptional zeal in seeking to promote union among Christians.

As early as 1634 he published a plan of union which he circulated among various Christian groups in Scotland, England, Germany, Transylvania, Sweden, and even to Denmark. Many of the continental reformed divines expressed favor to his plan of union and he also communicated this plan to leaders in New England who expressed a hearty approval of it. Richard Baxter observed: "'Mr. Dury having spent thirty years in his endeavors to reconcile the Lutherans and Calvinists, was again going abroad upon that work, and desired the judgment of our association how it might be most successfully accomplished."

With all the sharp controversies and eventual divisions among the reformed family, it is helpful to see that there were peace makers in the Assembly, John Dury being the foremost of them. Dury was a man of amiable character and greatly respected by those who disagreed with him. He indefatigably labored in the pursuit of Christian unity, taking to heart the scriptural admonition in Ephesians 4, which stresses that it is a diligent labor, requiring much work, to keep the unity of the gospel in the bond of peace. One of

Dury's letters to the Lord Chancellor Hide in July of 1660 summarizes his life's goal:

> My Lord, In the application which I made to your honor when you were at the Hague, I offered the fruit of my thirty years labors towards healing the breaches of Protestants; and this I did as one who never had served the turn of any party, or have been biased by particular interests for any advantage to myself; but walking in the light by rules and principles, have stood free from all in matters of strife, to be able to serve through love. My way hath been, and is, to solicit the means of peace and truth among the dissenting parties, to do good offices, and to quiet their discontents, and I must still continue in this way if I should be useful. But not being rightly understood in my aims and principles, I have been constrained to give this brief account thereof, as well to rectify the misconstructions of former actings, as to prevent farther mistakes concerning my way . . . and wherein I hope to persevere unto the end, as the Lord shall enable me, to be without offence unto all, with a sincere purpose to approve myself to his Majesty in all faithfulness.

Dury left behind several writings and his pursuit of unity did not discourage strength of principle. Advocating views which were quite uncompromising, Dury wrote *Of Presbytery and Independency* (1646), *Model of Church Government* (1647), and *Seasonable Discourse for Reformation* (1649). He also wrote *Peace-maker the Gospel Way* (1648), and his magnum opus, *The Unchanged, Constant, and Single-hearted Peace-maker drawn forth into the world: or, A Vindication of John Dury from the aspersions cast upon him in a nameless Pamphlet . . . (*1650). Dury provides us with an excellent example of a peace-maker in pursuit of a healthy peace. Most Christians today who still subscribe to the work of the Westminster Assembly, could also profit from remembering the peace-maker of the Westminster Assembly. "Blessed are the peace-makers."

Stephen Marshall

Stephen Marshall, born in Huntingdonshire, England and educated at Emmanuel College, was one of the finest preachers and leaders in early seventeenth century England. He was known as a "Reaper in God's Harvest" and Richard Baxter spoke of him as a "sober and worthy man." Marshall served as a minister at Finchingfield and was frequently called on to preach to the Long Parliament.

One biographer estimated his influence as a leader of the Assembly: "No man was more gracious . . . He was their trumpet, by whom they sounded their solemn Fasts, preaching more public sermons on that occasion, than any four of his [colleagues]. In their sickness he was their confessor, in their assembly their counselor, in their treaties their chaplain, in their disputations their champion." Clarendon says, "And without doubt, the Archbishop of Canterbury had never so great an influence upon the councils at court, as Mr. Marshall and Dr. Burgess had upon the Houses of Parliament." On one solemn Fasting Day before the House of Commons in 1640 it is reported that Dr. Burgess and Mr. Marshall preached at least seven hours, so intent were they to communicate the message of the cross.

In 1641, a pamphlet was published, in which defenders of the divine rule of presbyterianism debated the Anglican church's claim to priority. A written response to Bishop Hall's *Humble Remonstrance* (a work defending the episcopal form of government), was issued under the odd name of Smectymnuus. Later it was discovered that this latinism was an acronym, composed of letters from the names of 5 leading presbyterian co-authors in London: Stephen Marshall, Edmund Calamy, Thomas Young, Matthew Newcomen, and William Spurstow. Stephen Marshall was not only a great expositor, but an ecclesiastical churchman of mighty thought and conviction as well.

Stephen Marshall was the author with the first two initials in the <u>Smectymnuus</u> volume of 1641 which contended for Presbyterian government. Later he served as a chaplain to the Earl of Essex. Shortly after the Westminster Assembly convened, Stephen Marshall and Philip Nye were sent to escort the Scottish commissioners back to England, a duty which he served with joy. Marshall was also one of the first to argue for the institution of ruling elders by divine mandate. During the Assembly he assisted Robert Baillie in soliciting the support of foreign reformed churches in the British efforts to have a reformed Presbytery.

As one of the leaders urging the British Parliament to adopt the Solemn League and Covenant, the day after it was introduced Marshall co-wrote a letter which concluded with these sentiments: "We scarcely ever saw so much of Christ for us as this day, in the Assembly's carrying of this business, such weeping, such rejoicing, such resolution, such pathetical expressions, as we confess hath much refreshed our hearts, before extremely saddened with ill news from our dear country; and hath put us in good hope that this nation, which sets about this business, as becometh the work of God and saving of the kingdoms, shall be the means of lifting up distressed England and Ireland."

Marshall, "the preacher of the Assembly" was known as the best preacher in all of England. Moreover, despite his tendency to debate for an unlimited design to Christ's atonement (likely understood in light of his desire as a preacher to call all hearers to repentance), he was one of the doctrinal purists of the Assembly, even on occasion involving himself in publishing views which were contrary to the crown and considered subversive.

Marshall has been given various epitaphs which convey his colorful personality, variously having been called, "the great bell-weather of Presbyterians," "a famous incendiary, and assistant to the

Parliamentarians," "the Geneva-Bull, and a factious and rebellious divine," "and the Archflamen of the rebellious rout." Of his posthumous sermons and of his death itself it has been said, "'That he left behind him few laborers like himself; that he was a Christian in practice as well as in profession; that he lived by faith, and died by faith, and was an example to the believers, in word, in conversation, in charity, in faith, and in purity. . . . Respecting his death, he said, 'I cannot say, as one did, I have not so lived that I should now be afraid to die; but this I can say, I have so learned Christ, that I am not afraid to die.'" Marshall died in November of 1655 and left behind a number of writings, among which is his 1645 *A Defense of Infant Baptism* that was dedicated to the Assembly of divines and commissioners of the Church of Scotland then sitting at Westminster.

Herbert Palmer

Herbert Palmer (1601-1647) was perhaps unusual for an evangelical leader in that he came from a family of great wealth and nobility. He was nurtured in the faith by his parents and came to have a great love for scriptures in early childhood. He also learned French which would later be useful for him in his ministry. When he announced that he would become a minister, some of his friends sought to discourage him by telling him that ministers of Christ were hated, despised, and scourged. Young Palmer responded that that was no concern for him, for the love of God was more of his concern than the opinion of man. This was one minister who counted the costs before entering the ministry.

Accepted at Cambridge in 1615, he graduated with his Masters in 1622, and the following year became a fellow of Queen's College at Cambridge. He was ordained to the Gospel Ministry in 1624 at the age of 23. Later he would serve in the ministry at the Alphage Church in Canterbury beginning in 1626. On several occasions his small stature and youthful look led his audience to be surprised by the depths of his preaching and teaching ministry. Yet he was highly beneficial to many and his speech was like a disciple of Christ seasoned with grace, sweetness, and courtesy. Moreover, he also had a wide-spread ministry through his letters, by which he encouraged many Christians. On occasion he preached to the French congregation in Canterbury, drawing upon his earlier acquired fluency in French.

In 1632 he accepted a call to a church in Ashwell in Hartfordshire. His desire while in the ministry was to free his people from ignorance, and by his constant and zealous exposition, to have them intimately acquainted with their Bibles. While at Ashwell he published a catechism entitled, "An endeavor of making the Principles of the Christian Religion plain and easy" which was a proto-type of the Westminster Shorter Catechism; thus leading Palmer to be called the father of the Shorter Catechism.

Of Palmer it may be said, "True religion will be family religion." Palmer's family was exemplary and his house was characterized by an eminent sense of religion, so much so that his house was seen as a school of religion. He was regularly in family worship twice a day, not excusing family members from worship. He also catechized his own family twice a week. After every meal his servants had some portion of Scripture and part of some major religious treatise read to them.

In 1632 he became one of the preachers to the university of Cambridge serving as a chaplain with Dr. Tuckney. In 1640 he became a pastor of New Church, Westminster. In 1644 Herbert Palmer was elected as a master of Queen's College under the sponsorship of the Earl of Manchester. In this role of administrative leadership for the college he was very careful to maintain that no person should be admitted to scholarship or fellowship whose clear profession of faith was not evident.

Herbert Palmer wrote a number of books, such as *Of Making Religion One's Business*. Palmer inherited a large estate, yet he chose a humble life to serve his Master, maintaining and sponsoring several poor scholars of his own while they were studying to show themselves approved. While faithfully participating in the Westminster Assembly, he frequently preached to Parliament, stating that honor in this way: "that he did not in that place preach before them, *as before a judge*, but to them authoritatively, as by commission from God. And how much soever they might be superior to him in other respects, yet he was in that place superior to them, as acting in God's name; and therefore would not be afraid to speak, whatever was the will of God and he should tell them, notwithstanding any displeasure or danger which might by this means befall him for so doing." Palmer no doubt knew our Lord's words" "When you are brought before . . . rulers and authorities . . . the Holy Spirit will teach you what you should say" (Lk. 12:12).

Lazarus Seaman

Born in Leicester, England and educated at Emmanuel College, Lazarus Seaman was the opposite of Herbert Palmer. Seaman came to school penniless and had to drop out of school temporarily to teach in order to make his living. He was self-taught and was part-time Chaplain to the Earl of Northumberland. In 1642 he was ordained and served as Pastor of Allhallows in London. Of him a contemporary said, "He was a person of a most deep, piercing, and eagle-eyed judgment in all points of controversial divinity. He had few equals, if any superiors, in ability to decide and determine a dark and doubtful controversy. He could state a theological question with admirable clearness and acuteness, and knew how, in a controversy, to cleave, as we say, a hair. Nor was he less able to defend than to find out the truth.'"

He was so respected in debate that sometimes his opponents were disheartened upon seeing his name on the list of speakers. In 1644 he was master at the university of Cambridge and took a public declaration of his desire to see the niversituy reformed: "I do solemnly and seriously promise, in the presence of Almighty God, the Searcher of all hearts, that, during the time of my continuance in that charge, I shall faithfully labor to promote piety and learning in myself, the fellows, scholars, and students, who do or shall belong to the said College, agreeably to the late solemn national league and covenant . . . and by all means to procure the welfare, and perfect reformation both of that College and University, so far as to me appertains."

He was known for his polemical divinity and his excellence as a good expositor of the Holy Scriptures. He was ejected in the Act of Uniformity in 1662 and of him it was said, "I never admired his scholarship so much as I did his patience, the lesson in which he grew so perfect in the School of affliction. . . . Dr. Seaman was a burning and shining light; . . . a scribe instructed to the kingdom of heaven, like a man who is an householder, who bringeth out of his treasure things new and old. I may justly say of him, that he was an ocean of Theology, and that he had so thoroughly digested the whole body of divinity, that he could upon all occasions discourse upon any point without labor. He was a living body of Divinity, and his tongue as the pen of a ready writer. He was a person of great stability and steadiness in the truth. I am confident that he valued one truth of Christ, above all the wealth of both the Indies.—He was deeply and tenderly sensible of the state of the church of Christ. He was ever very inquisitive how it fared with the people of God in foreign parts; and this not out of Athenian curiosity, but out of a public spirit of Christianity . . . Industrious and indefatigable in his Calling—Admirably prudent both in his speech and behavior—And an example of patience in suffering affliction."

Anthony Tuckney

Anthony Tuckney (1599-1670) was one of the few divines to have communication with the American colonies in New England. Born into a minister's family in Lincolnshire, Tuckney was educated at Emmanuel College, Cambridge. Following his graduation he tutored many students who later became quite useful in both church and state. His first ministerial assignment was to serve as the Assistant to the famous John Cotton, minister of Boston. In 1633, John Cotton resigned his pastorate in England and went to New England, with Tuckney succeeding him as pastor in Boston, England. Communications with Cotton would be one of the few direct sources of feedback between Old England and New England.

At the Westminster Assembly, Tuckney was so respected that he served on the most important committees—the Committee for examination of prospective ministers and the Committee of Accommodation—to seek to reconcile the differing views of the various parties. He also had a primary role in developing the Confession of Faith and Catechisms. It is thought that many of the answers in the larger Catechism, especially in the wording of the exposition of the Law, are derived from his fertile mind.

He later served as Pastor of Michael-Queen church in London, and became a Master (Professor) of Emmanuel College in 1645, becoming the Vice-Chancellor of the college in 1648. Tuckney had an illustrious academic career, being appointed Master of St. John's College in 1653, and succeeding the eminent Dr. Arrowsmith as Royal Professor, while at the same time retaining his great humility.

This covenantal discipler took those things he had heard and passed them on to faithful students, who in turn would pass them on to others (2 Tim. 2:2).

In 1662, he was ejected with his other fellow ministers in the Act of Uniformity and died in 1670 at the age of 71. He left behind a number of written works, among them a collection of 40 sermons, published posthumously (1676) and a Latin dissertation against spreading religion by the coercive power of the sword, which was poorly received in his native England, but published in Holland (1679).

Tuckney was a respected leader at the Assembly, and being sure of his convictions, frequently helped the bogged-down convocation move to a vote on the questions. He was an ardent presbyterian.

Richard Vines

Richard Vines (1600-1655), following his graduation from Magdalen College, Cambridge, began his service to the Lord as an educator, serving as schoolmaster at Hinckley in Leicestershire. His first parish was at Weddington, a private village in Warwickshire, where he also faithfully served the small adjacent church at Caldcot until 1642. At the outbreak of the civil war, he also established a public discussion at Nuneaton, seven miles from Coventry, where many travelled to hear his exposition. Both evangelism and edification were united in these lectures.

An expert in matters of church government, Vines was called "the champion of the party in the Assembly, therefore called their Luther." Later he was called to minister to the large parish of Clement's Danes, whose parishioners included the Earl of Essex, a life-long friend. Vines gave the funeral oration at the Earl's death, perhaps at that time speaking to the largest number of influential people in his entire ministry.

In 1644 Vines was appointed Professor of Pembroke-Hall, Cambridge, where he served until 1649. At the Assembly, Vines also served on the Committee of Accommodation and in 1645 was appointed to the committee to prepare the Confession of Faith. One biographer said of him:

> He was mighty in the Scriptures, and an interpreter one of a thousand. He was a great champion in controversy, and eminently distinguished for giving a mortal wound to error. In his powerful

and spiritual ministry, he insisted every much upon the all-important doctrine of justification, which he had thoroughly studied; greatly debasing man and exalting the Lord Jesus Christ, and his finished righteousness. Toward the conclusion of his ministry, he discovered much earnestness, in driving man out of himself unto the Savior; throwing down all false foundations of the hope of heaven, and warmly recommending the only sure foundation which Jehovah has laid in Zion. He seriously exhorted his hearers to study heart-holiness and a conversation becoming the gospel of Christ. And he knew well how to speak a word in season to wounded spirits.

He died in middle age, with a severe affliction and great suffering. leaving behind a reputation for excellence as an expert in the original language of the New Testament. He was known as "the very prince of preachers, a thorough Calvinist, and a bold honest man, without pride and flattery." So respected was he that at his death some 13 funeral poems or elegies were composed. One funeral elegy noted the following:

Our English Luther, Vines, whose death I weep,
Stole away (and said nothing) in a sleep.
Sweet (like a swan) he preached the day he went,
And for his cordial took a sacrament;
Had it but been suspected he would die,
His people sure had stopped him with their cry.

Quite a witness. In addition, his chief written works were a *Treatise on the Sacrament of the Lord's Supper*, a collection of 20 sermons on the subject, and devotional works such as *Christ the Christian's only Gain* (1661), *God's Drawing and Man's Coming to Christ* (1662), and *The Saint's Nearness to God* (1662). Having been justified by faith, he had peace with God.

Samuel Rutherford

Samuel Rutherford (1600-1661) was born in southern Scotland and graduated from Edinburgh University in 1621, where he subsequently served as professor of classical languages. He later served in Anwoth, Scotland as a pastor until 1636 and was very active in local ministry while he continued his studies. In 1636 he was deposed from office for non-conformity to the Church of England and spent two years in confinement. While incarcerated, Rutherford, not only a man of prayer but also one of determination, composed several works in his memory, even at times writing on the walls of his cells with a coal or on the windows with a point of a pin.

Upon his release from prison in 1638 he was restored to his flock at Anwoth and shortly thereafter was appointed as a Professor of Divinity in the New College of Edinburgh. Rutherford was also a signer of the 1638 Solemn League and Covenant, and so esteemed for his orthodoxy that, in 1643, he was appointed to be a commissioner at the Westminster Assembly. Rutherford's debates and instruction at this Assembly were most appreciated and helpful. Often drawing upon rabbinic writings, and even upon occasion debating with the esteemed Lightfoot with some success, Rutherford was a definite contributor to that Assembly.

It was during this London period in the mid 1640s that Rutherford was a prolific author of books on church discipline. Rutherford wrote a number of treatises, including *A Peaceable and Temperate Plea for Paul's Presbytery in Scotland* (1642) and *The Due Right of Presbyteries* in 1644. It was also in 1644 that his classic *Lex Rex* was published, followed in 1652 by his *Divine Right of Church Government and Excommunication*. Rutherford was an expert both in matters of church polity, and also in theology. He wrote a number of works disputing the claims of the Arminians and in 1648 was even offered an invitation to take up the Chair of Divinity at the University of Utrecht in Holland. Nonetheless, he remained at the University of Edinburgh in 1649 and taught there for many years. With the Restoration of Charles II in 1660, Rutherford and many of the other covenanters were in danger. Rutherford was one of the first ministers summoned to meet with these leaders of the Restoration and in October of 1660 his books were burned in front of the castle of Edinburgh. It was commonly said that it was much easier to burn his books than to answer them. His trial continued and, called to appear before the higher tribunal in March of 1661, by God's grace Rutherford's sentence was commuted by his death on March 29, 1661.

William Twisse

The man who became the first moderator of the Assembly had a long and distinguished career in ministry. Described as a "venerable man, with the long, pale countenance, imposing beard, lofty brow, and meditative eye," he has often been miscast, or remained unknown. William Twisse of Newbury was a scholar and devout man of God. Shortly after the Long Parliament took power (Nov. 3, 1640), the members of Parliament called for a preliminary meeting with "learned divines" to be briefed. Among the participants in this warm-up for the Assembly were Archbishop Ussher, William Twisse, and a few others. Thus, far before the Assembly, Twisse had established his reputation as one of the leading biblical teachers of his day. He was known as a deep and often speculative genius. Baxter describes him as "a man very famous for his Scholastical Wit and Writings in a very smooth triumphant stile."

In addition, his potency as a controversialist and defender of the reformed faith was widely known. He was a one-man Arminian-buster, known for his subtle and logical prowess. Thomas Fuller eulogized his abilities in these words: ". . . a divine of great abilities, learning, piety, and moderation... His plain preaching was good, his disputing better, his pious living best of all . . . Good with the trowel, but better with the sword, more happy in polemical divinity than edifying doctrine." While characterized by theological precision, Twisse's participation in the Assembly is a model of irenic spirit, absent of that quarrelsomeness which so often accompanies depth of theological conviction.

Twisse was also known for his own prayer life and family

devotionals. One biographer reported: "Always before dinner. . . , he read a portion of the holy scriptures, expounding the more obscure and difficult passages, for the edification of the family . . . that their souls might be refreshed along with their bodies; that they might see themselves in the glass of the divine law; become better acquainted with the Word of God, . . . and talk of all his wondrous works."

According to participant Robert Baillie, Twisse was an excellent and even-handed moderator. Even if appointed by those "who guide most matters for their own interests," Moderator Twisse proved a valuable gift to fairness and efficiency. He is described by Baillie as one who "the world knows, is very learned in the questions he has studied; and very good, and beloved of all, and highly esteemed."

Not one to seek prominence, hardly could an assignment have been given which was so unsolicited. Twisse humbly thought himself more suited for other tasks, and "Unskilled in parliamentary law, diffident of his own judgment, incapable of strong self-assertion, dreamy and absent-minded in the midst of the long debates, he strove to do his duty in an office which he would have been only too glad to demit." When it is recalled that Twisse was perhaps a stricter Calvinist than some, and yet that the Confession does not reflect his particular views, it becomes clear that Twisse was a moderator who did not seek to inject his own personal views or idiosyncracies on the Assembly, certainly an admirable trait, as well as a potent rebuttal to those who venomously accuse the Assembly of intolerance.

The last known act at the Assembly was his signature of a petition to Parliament, apparently in response to the latest Erastian initiatives of Selden, in which Twisse and other divines contended eloquently for the freedom of the church, apart from state interference or control. Twisse's piety was also well known, as he would frequently call on members to pray or give a word of exhortation, even on occasion referring to the agreement as a "sweet concurrence." Witherspoon reports that Twisse died while praying, and that immediately prior to hearing that his end was near, smiled with confidence and said, "Now, at length, I shall have leisure to follow my studies to all eternity."

Lord Warriston

Archibald Johnstone, who later became known as Lord Warriston was a rising legal star in Scotland, when Charles I sought to impose formality in worship and hierarchical rule in the church. A godly ruling elder with legal background, sound judgment, talent in negotiation, and commitment to religious freedom, Johnstone became a leader in the reform of the Scottish church. When the General Assembly of Scotland met in 1638 in Glasgow to frame what would come to be known as the Solemn League and Covenant, Johnstone was unanimously chosen to be clerk of the Assembly. At the young age of 27, this shrewd lawyer, who was "apt to forget time on his knees, a man of power with his brethren," would become one of the top leaders in the Scottish church, along with Henderson. A fellow Scottish historian spoke of Warriston as "in heart and soul a Covenanter on religious, not political principles; from which he never swerved."

Prior to this the King had sought to induce Johnstone to favor his causes by elevating Johnstone to the order of Knighthood, even installing him as a Judge. But even with the addition of the title "Lord Warriston," still Johnstone valued faithfulness to the covenant more than the advancement that an earthly king could bring. Hetherington summarized his character: "In the Westminster Assembly Warriston attended very constantly, and frequently engaged in the discussions and debates of that grave and learned body, fully maintaining his high reputation. Even the English Parliament requested him to sit among them and aid in their deliberations, although he was not, and could not become, a member of that high court. Along with Henderson, Warriston became known as one of the eminent Scottish churchmen."

At a crucial juncture in the Assembly in 1646, while discussing the right of the church to be free from state control, Warriston addressed the Assembly and Parliament. Listen in at mid-speech:

> ... for the highest end—the settling the crown of Christ in this island to be propagat[ed] from island to continent. Until King Jesus be set down on his throne with his sceptre in his hand I do not expect God's peace, and so no solid peace from men in these kingdomes; but that soveraigne truth being established a durable peace will be found to follow hereupon.... Sir, this should teach us to be as tender, zealous, and carefull to assert Christ and his Church their priviledge and right, and to forewarn all least they endanger your souls ... Christ lives and reigns alone over and in his Church, and will have all done therein according to his Word and will, and that he hes given no supreme headship over his Church to any pope, king, or parliament whatsoever.... Christ is a king and has a kingdome in the externall government of his church, and that he has set doun the lawes and offices and other substantialls thereof. Wee must not now before men mince, hold up, conceal, prudentially waive anything necessary for this testimony, ... nor edge away an hem of Christ's robe royal. These would seem effects of desertions, tokens of being ashamed, affrayed, or politikly diverted, ...

Such was the combination of bravery and insight. On the restoration of Charles II orders were issued for the seizure of others, including Warriston, but he escaped and fled to the continent. "While there, he was attacked by a severe illness, and reduced almost to death by that and the unskillfulness—some say the treachery—of a physician. From the prostration of all bodily and even mental power, caused by this illness and treatment, he never wholly recovered. The cold, revengeful eye of Charles was still upon him; and in 1663 he was seized in France, brought to Scotland, tried, condemned, and executed, when so enfeebled by age and disease that he could scarcely either stand or speak. Yet with the calm tranquility and spiritual elevation of a martyr, he gave the relics of his wasted life to the cause in which he had strenuously expended his strength."

George Gillespie

George Gillespie, was the youngest member of the Assembly and also one of the shortest-lived. Born in 1613 to the Rev. John Gillespie, a Minister at Kirkcaldy, he began his academic studies in 1629 at St. Andrews. Being convinced at an early age, and ahead of his other peers (e.g., Baillie and Henderson) that episcopacy was a human invention, he courageously refused episcopal ordination. As early as 1637, when Gillespie was a mere 24, he authored his first book, *A Dispute against the English Popish Ceremonies,* which quickly established young Gillespie as an astute theological mind, and force to be reckoned with., a genius, some would say. In this work, he systematically and biblically refuted the episcopal claims point by point.

Shortly thereafter, the power of the bishops waned, and Gillespie was ordained by the Presbytery of Kirkcaldy on April 26, 1638, having been called to the parish of Wemyss. Fittingly, he was the first to be admitted by a presbytery in that period without ordination by bishops, courageously practicing what he preached. In 1642, he moved to Edinburgh to accept a call, and arrived at the Westminster Assembly, with Henderson as the first rank of Scottish Presbyterians on Sept. 15, 1643, at the ripe age of 30, in the fifth year of his ordained ministry.

Of his abilities, contemporary Robert Baillie described Gillespie as that 'noble youth':

That is an excellent youth; my heart blessed God in his behalf. There is no man whose parts in public dispute I do so admire. He has studied so accurately all the points that are yet come to our Assembly; he has got so ready, so assured, so solid a way of public debating; that however there be in the Assembly divers excellent men, yet, in my poor judgment, there is not one who speaks more rationally, and to the point, than that brave youth has done ever; so that his absence would be prejudicial to our whole cause, and unpleasant to all here that wishes it well.

So combined was intellect, godliness, and youthful lack of trepidation. He also authored other major works in presbyterian polity, and in 1647 when the Scottish Assembly adopted the Westminster Confession of Faith, they also printed Gillespie's *One Hundred and Eleven Propositions*, which were aimed at refuting Erastianism. The following year Gillespie was elected Moderator, at age 35 being one of the youngest Moderators of any Presbyterian body ever. It was fortunate too, as he would not live to see another Assembly, dying a premature and noble death on Dec. 17, 1648. Hetherington eulogized that he was "one of those bright and powerful spirits which are sent in troublous times to carry forward God's work among mankind, and recalled to heaven when that work is done." Hetherington also lavished this praise: "George Gillespie was one of that peculiar class of men who start like meteors into sudden splendor, shine with dazzling brilliancy, then suddenly set behind the tomb, leaving their compeers equally to admire and to deplore."

He was called a "Singular ornament of our Church, than whom not one in the whole Assembly speaks to a better purpose." Although the youngest member of the Assembly by far, he nearly single-handedly led the debates on government—both against some of the world's best apologists for Erastianism (e. g., Selden and Lightfoot), and independency (Goodwin and Nye). At a strategic moment, an elder Scots statesman as much as yielded the floor to the younger Gillespie. Following Selden's learned speech:

Then Samuel Rutherford turned eagerly and appealingly to young

Gillespie, and said, 'Rise, George, rise up, man, and defend the right of the Lord Jesus Christ to govern by his own laws the Church he has purchased with his blood.' George rose, calm, steady, and confident. It was a tremendous hour and a tremendous undertaking for a young man of thirty-one to answer Selden. But the stripling knew what he had in his sling. He answered Selden so effectually, so crushingly, that the giant was silenced. He is reported to have said, 'That young man has by a single speech swept away the learning and labor of ten years of my life.'

Surmises Beveridge: "When the Assembly met, he was little more than thirty; in five years his meteoric career had closed. In that short time his work was done, and wonderfully done. 'With the fire of youth he had the wisdom of age.'"

Alexander Henderson

I begin this study in character at mid-stream with a vignette of bravery. On an earlier occasion Henderson was moderating a Scottish Assembly, whose express purpose was to abolish the Scottish episcopacy. Charles I sent to this venerable body a distinguished soldier, the Marquis of Hamilton, with the king's authority to dissolve the Assembly should it attempt to annul the episcopacy. As Henderson and the other Scottish presbyters called for the Bishops' resignations, the Marquis of Hamilton paraded in, in full military dress and held a conspicuous seat in the front of the meeting room. Witherspoon takes the story from here.

> The answer of the bishops having been read, Mr. Henderson, with that stately dignity and overawing gravity which were characteristic of him, arose and asked if it was the pleasure of the Assembly to proceed to the trial of the bishops. On this the Marquis of Hamilton sprang to his feet and declared that it was not in accordance with the pleasure of his majesty, King Charles, . . . and he was present in the king's name to interdict any proceedings in that direction.

Alexander Henderson then calmly thanked the Marquis, assured him of their intent to conform themselves to the king's will as far as possible, but further reminded him that these commissioners had a higher loyalty, with their first allegiance to the universal Sovereign. As Moderator, he then put the question to the Assembly. The

Marquis of Hamilton, astonished to be sure, warned that such would be considered revolutionary. Henderson calmly stuck to his guns, and put the question a third time.

At this the loyal soldier rose and declared that if another word on this subject was uttered he would dissolve the meeting. Henderson, composed, sought once again to reassure the Marquis. However, at that moment the soldier sprang to the front and declared the Assembly dissolved on the authority of the king. After charging each member to have no more to do with this, the soldier "stalked down the aisle and out of the door, his sabre rattling behind him." Let Witherspoon describe the closing act.

> When the door had closed, Mr. Henderson's wonderful self-possession and genius appeared. Calming the turbulence of the excited throng that was ready to pursue the Marquis with personal violence, Mr. Henderson commended him for his fidelity to his sovereign, and for carrying out the instructions given him to the letter; then, turning, reminded the Assembly that they were commissioners of a greater King, and urged them by the example of the king's servant and representative, to obey, even to the death, the inspired and authoritative instructions of King Jesus. The effect was magnetic; the bishops were brought to the bar, convicted of contumacy, and deposed, Mr. Henderson conducting the ceremony of deposition amidst a solemnity and awe that would have befitted the judgment day.

Alexander Henderson, one of the leading Scottish commissioners at the Westminster Assembly, was born in 1583. He entered St. Andrews in 1599, receiving his degree in 1603. Henderson likely heard the final lectures of the aged Andrew Melville at St. Andrews, thus providing a link to Knox and the other original reformers. Shortly after graduation, he was appointed Professor of philosophy and rhetoric at St. Andrews, where he served until 1613. At that time, he was nominated by Archbishop Gladstone to serve the parish of Leuchars. Interestingly at that time, Henderson, who would later become a stalwart defender of presbyterianism, approved of the episcopacy.

At his ordination, so opposed was he by the parishioners, that he arrived early at the Leuchars church, and locked all the doors, lest the crowd seek to overturn his installation. Then he and the other clergy climbed in through the window to hold the ordination service, an incident which would later loom large in Henderson's conversion. A little later, the eminent preacher, Robert Bruce of Kinnaird was in the area, and Henderson went to hear him. As the Spirit would have it, Bruce preached on John 15, where Jesus said, "I say unto you, He that entereth not by the door, but climbeth up some other way, the same is a Thief and a Robber." These words were so convicting that they led to Henderson's conversion. Following that, he went back and re-examined the biblical basis for church government, and became a convinced presbyterian.

A leader among the Council which drew up the National Covenant, Henderson was present, with sixty thousand other Presbyterians, who gathered at Edinburgh to adopt the Solemn League and Covenant. In fact, Henderson opened the meeting at Grey Friars in prayer at 2 o'clock in the afternoon. The covenant was then read, and according to tradition, some signed with their own blood, and confirmed the covenant by oath.

After being besieged by a petition, the King finally relented and called for a General Assembly, the first in 20 years, to be held at St. Mungo's Cathedral in Glasgow on Nov. 21, 1638. With many a dignitary, even Dukes and The Lord High Commissioner, and ruling elders who really ruled (bearing arms for enforcement, if needed), Henderson was elected Moderator. One of the first and most decisive acts of this Assembly was to depose the bishops, which took place, Dec. 13th, after Henderson preached on "The Lord said unto my Lord, Sit thou on my right hand, till I make thine enemies thy footstool." Following the sermon, with solemnity and gravity, Henderson pronounced the sentence of deposition. As a Moderator, Henderson constitutionally deposed 2 archbishops, 12 bishops (of whom 8 were excommunicated as well).

In 1641, again Henderson was made Moderator, and by this time was not only a religious leader, but a civil leader as well. In 1642, Henderson was assigned the responsibility of answering a letter from the Parliament of England as to the feasibility of a joint meeting to further reformation teaching and practice in the three countries. Henderson proposed that they do so along the lines of the Scottish Solemn league and Covenant (1638), to which the British Parliament consented. Henderson was thus the principal author of the framework for the calling and purpose of the Westminster Assembly.

His statesmanship is still a model. Says Hetherington: "Henderson was by nature a king of men, and his whole bearing and language were always kingly. He was one of those great men whom God gives to elevate a nation, and work a mighty work; and whose departure leaves that age dark, feeble, and deploring". He exhibited "unremitting devotion to the cause of truth," and "in the furnace of controversy, Henderson never departed from the gentle courtesy which becomes the servant of the Lord. In the great emergencies of the conflict between truth and error he saw what ought to be done and did it. When a course of action was once determined upon, he followed it strenuously and persistently until the result was secured." He ruled, as Moderator with "a hand of steel in a velvet glove," and was "the destroyer in Scotland of a church government alien to the faith and spirit of the people; as the penman of the Solemn League and Covenant; as the proposer of the Westminster Assembly; as the leading commissioner of the Church of Scotland in that great body; as the friend of the kin; as the unifier of the forces of righteousness and order in the Church and State, he stands a man whose like either Church or State have seldom known."

His colleague Baillie eulogized him as "that glorious soul of worthy memory, who is now crowned with the reward of his labors for God and for us, . . . fragrant among us so long as pure and free Assemblies remain in this land, which I hope will be till the coming of the Lord." Another said that Henderson ". . . perhaps ranks next to John Knox in our Scottish history . . . the fairest ornament, after Mr. John Knox, of incomparable memory, that ever the Church of Scotland did enjoy."

Sadly, he lived to view the re-imposition of the episcopacy in Scotland, dying heart-broken in August 1646 that the desired reform was not taking deeper root. In 1898, historian William Henry Roberts assessed: "In this land [USA], further, the popular government which Henderson loved, and which finds its roots in the Calvinistic system, has come to full development. Do you ask for one monument of Henderson and his colaborers, look upon the Republic, free, united, prosperous. Do you ask for another, look upon the Presbyterian churches of this land, loyal to the core, despite all opposition, to the truth of God."

"His writings, his speeches, are all characterized by calmness and ease, without the slightest appearance of heat or agitation; — resulting unquestionably from that aspect of character generally termed *greatness of mind*; but which would in him be more properly characterized by describing it as a rare combination of intellectual power, moral dignity, and spiritual elevation. It was the condition of a mighty mind, enjoying the peace of God which passeth understanding,—a peace which the world had not given, and could not take away." (Hetherington, p. 146) In 1943 as a portrait of Henderson was being dedicated, William C. Gray noted that "we make too little of the 'living epistles' sent of God to us from age to age in the persons" (*Anniversary Addresses,* p. 39.) of our heroes.

Westminster Spirituality

The claim that the authors of the Westminster Confession were spiritual giants may be met either with looks of horror, disbelief, shock, or even bursts of laughter. Sadly, few moderns are aware of the depth and breadth of spirituality in these divines. Our unawareness of this is both our own loss and due to no fault of the divines. The footprints of their spirituality are not beyond tracing out.

Perhaps only an age like our own—which so loathes so much of the past—would make this mistake. However, Christians should have broader horizons than the narrow confines of any single age, and saints should desire to benefit from the examples of those who have gone before them. Indeed, a perennial challenge is to identify mentors or to emulate those whose spirituality surpasses our own. I modestly suggest that we begin our search for such spiritual role models, not so much with our own contemporaries as we are inclined to do but with some who may have superseded our own spirituality. It may be put this way: If we desire to imitate the best of orthodox spirituality, why not study the lives and practices of the best of Christians? Until we surpass the divines of Westminster in spirituality, until our age on the whole possesses more innate spiritual vitality, until we find deeper and cooler wells of spiritual refreshment, why not draw the contours of spirituality from the lives and spiritual disciplines of these divines?

If we have ears to hear we can garner some of the richest

testimonies from real Christians of an earlier age. In fact, these testimonies are more God-centered and dripping with grace-filled piety than many of the standard testimonies we hear today. Not to disparage any modern testimonies, but the truth of the matter is that those Puritans on the average were more—not less—advanced than the average evangelical today.

Critics of Westminster Spirituality

Critics, of course, would be hesitant to agree with our study. Certain persons and images from the past sometimes stand in dire need of rehabilitation. The divines, too, suffer outside the camp as some of the most maligned in history, being ranked with the likes of Calvin, Beza, Turretin, and a few others. Sadly, most of the modern world (and it should not be so in an informed church) think of these divines as machine-tooled, robo-theologians, bereft of heart, passion, emotion, and maybe even soul. That is a caricature underivable from the best historical review. Images accumulated through history are often hard to jettison, even if those accrued images are not in accord with actual history. Unfortunately, the divines of Westminster have been tarred and feathered (normally by opponents) to the point that they are seldom recommended as worthwhile models of spiritual fervor or compassion. They have frequently been caricatured as "black hats" by those who did not understand or agree with them. With even the slightest archaeological digging, however, one can see that these men—far from being spiritually sterile—evinced a spirituality of the highest order. It is not the case that these divines were spiritual pygmies. It is time to help rehabilitate these saints. Any who slander them without reviewing the record first are guilty of false witness not to mention ignorance. These divines were deeply spiritual; most of us could learn from them.

Of the Westminster Confession of Faith as an accurate and vital compilation of Christian truth, B. B. Warfield contended that its influence could not "lack in spiritual quality. . . . [Its] authors were men of learning and philosophic grasp; but above all of piety.

Their interest was not in speculative construction, but in the protection of their flocks from deadly error."[1]

On the group as a whole, biographer James Reid commented:

> There were never, perhaps, men of holier lives than the generality of the Puritans and Nonconformists of this period. Their piety and devotedness to God were very remarkable. Their ministers made considerable sacrifices for God and religion. They spent their lives, in sufferings, in fastings, in prayers, in walking closely with God in their families, and among their people who were under their pastoral care, in a firm adherence to their principles, and in a series of unremitted labors for the good of mankind. They were indefatigably zealous in their Master's service.[2]

Many of the critics' barbs must first be dismissed if we are to benefit from the example of these saints. For example, Sidney Ahlstrom marveled, "That so many learned and contentious men in an age of so much theological hair-splitting could with so little coercion establish so resounding a consensus on so detailed a doctrinal statement is one of the marvels of the century."[3] Criticism of the divines as precisionists is certainly not exclusively a modern sport.

A great tradition of slandering the divines exists. In his 1647 burlesque, *The Assembly-Man*,[4] John Birkenhead (1616-1679) illustrates the accusation of the divines for intolerance: "The only difference 'twixt the Assembler and a Turk, is, that one plants Religion by the power of the Sword, and the other by the power of the scimitar." He proceeded to allege, "Nay, the greatest strife in

---

[1] Cited in W. G. T. Shedd, *Calvinism: Pure and Mixed* (rpr. Edinburgh: Banner of Truth Trust, 1986), p. 161.
[2] James Reid, *Memoirs of the Westminster Assembly of Divines* (Edinburgh: Banner of Truth Trust, 1982), p. 130.
[3] Sydney Ahlstrom, *A Religious History of the American People* (New York: Doubleday, 1975), vol. I, p. 136.
[4] Found in *Journal of Presbyterian History*, vol. xxi, nos. 2 and 3, June and September, 1943, pp. 133-147.

their whole Conventicle, is who shall do worst; for they all intend to make the Church but a Sepulchre, having not onely plundered, but anatomized all the true Clergy."[5]

Thus, these godly men were unfortunately but frequently accused of intolerance and the desire to seize power to persecute their opponents. In response, Hetherington wisely noted "that both the principles and the constitution of a rightly formed Presbyterian Church render the usurpation of power and the exercise of tyranny on its part wholly impossible."

Fairborn alleged that "to the Presbyterians, toleration was the very man of sin" and Masson, Milton's biographer, accused the Assembly as follows: "Toleration to them was a demon, a chimera, the Great Diana of the Independents."[6] They were also accused of immoderation in their pursuit to elucidate so many biblical truths. However, the Confession of Faith is quite moderate and non-inventive in its formulation of biblical truth.

The Assembly's moderation is evident in its refusal to settle the speculative controversy about the order of God's decrees in salvation (lapsarianism), instead allowing those debatable matters to be settled in other forums. Although the moderator (Twisse) had well-formed opinions on this subject, such specificity is not reflected in the Confession. Rather than staking out absolutist positions on every subject, this Assembly was guided by the biblical mandate of moderation. The Confession does not lay out an elaborate end-time scheme nor treat complex ethical issues. Neither does it attempt to settle all conceivable issues. It is restrained and moderate in scope. Still, criticisms endure.

John Milton even roasted the divines in his most famous epic. One scene from *Paradise Lost* was based on the sitting of the Assembly, as angry Milton compared the divines with the fallen angels in the infernal world. Milton likely had the Assembly in mind when he wrote:

---

[5] *Journal of Presbyterian History*, vol. xxi, nos. 2 and 3, p. 140.
[6] William Beveridge, *A Short History of the Westminster Assembly* (1904; rpr. Greenville, SC: A Press, 1991), p. 86.

Others, apart, sat on a hill retired,
In thought more elevate, and reasoned high

Of Providence, foreknowledge, will and fate;
Fixed fate, free will, foreknowledge absolute;
    And found no end, in wandering mazes lost.[7]

Similar doggerl was composed for the Synod as well:

Pretty Synod doth it sit,
Void of grace, as well of wit, . . .
    Thereby to end us;
From Synod's nonsense and their treason,
And from their catechistic reason,
    Good heaven, defend us![8]

Birkenhead the Royalist sympathizer was one of the most stinging critics of the Assembly. While the Assembly was sitting, his anonymously published tract, *The Assembly-Man*, broadcast vitriolic contempt for the Assembly. Birkenhead alleged that they sat "four years towards a new Religion, but in the interim left none at all."[9] Moreover, he esteemed the divines as "[a]toms; petty small Levites, whose parts are not perceptible . . . [who] follow the Geneva Margin, as those Seamen who understand not the Compass crept along the shore."[10]

Birkenhead assessed the Shorter Catechism as "paultry," accused the divines of being materially motivated, only interested in "silver chains," and satirized that "though the Assembler's Brains are Lead, his Countenance is Brass; for he condemned such as held two Benefices, while he himself has four or five, besides his Concubin-Lecture."[11] Contemporary critics did not avoid

---

[7] Cited in *Memorial Volume of the Westminster Assembly, 1647-1897*, ed. by Francis Beattie, Charles Hemphill, and Henry Escott (Richmond: Presbyterian Committee for Publication, 1897), p. 81.
[8] Cited in *Memorial Volume*, p. 81.
[9] Cf. *Journal of Presbyterian History*, vol. xxi, nos. 2 and 3, p. 137.
[10] Ibid., p. 138.

personal criticism. Assembly divine John Arrowsmith, an eminent Professor at Cambridge, along with his fellow-assemblymen, was castigated as follows: "So that Learning now is so much advanced, as Arrowsmith's Glass-eye sees more than his Natural."[12]

The Puritan traits of the divines were mocked, and they were charged with effeminacy: "His [a divine] two longest things are his Nails and his Prayer. But the cleanest thing about him is his Pulpit cushion, for he still beats the dust out of it."[13] Of the Puritan long-windedness, Birkenhead ridiculed a divine: "Yet though you heard him three hours, he'll ask a fourth, . . . If he has got any new Tale or Expression, 'tis easier to make Stones speak than him to hold his peace. He hates a Church where there is an Echo for it robs him of his dear Repetition, and confounds the Auditory as well as he." Of their sermons Birkenhead alleged that "had they the art to shorten it into Sense, they might write his whole Sermon on the back of their Nail."[14] Bitter criticisms were often set forth, citing the divines as the dupes of Parliament: "At Fasts and Thanksgivings the Assembler is the States' Trumpet; . . . proclaim News, very loud, the Trumpet and his Forehead both of one metal."[15]

Birkenhead's summation of the character of the divines was that they had "the Pride of three Tyrants, the Forehead of six Gaolers, and the Fraud of twelve Brokers. Or take him in the Bunch, and their whole Assembly is a Club of Hypocrites, where six dozen schismatics spend two hours for four shillings apiece."[16]

Is this an accurate description of their spirituality or is it a caricature? If accurate, then by all means these lives should not be spiritual guides. But if inaccurate, perhaps we can learn from these. Whatever the conclusion, it is important for anyone claiming the heritage of Westminster to do so without naiveté. While exposure

---

[11] Ibid., p. 139.
[12] Ibid., p. 141.
[13] Ibid., p. 142.
[14] Ibid., p. 145.
[15] Ibid., p. 146.
[16] Ibid., p. 147.

to criticism can help us avoid idolizing Westminster, exposure to history can help us avoid the groundless presumption that we are superior.

The Spirituality of the Westminster Assembly

This survey briefly considers the following traits of Westminster piety: fasting, spiritual warfare, preaching, confession of sins, testimonies about the family's nurture of children, as well as missionary zeal, reliance on Scripture, and last breath testimonies of faith from the lips of these seventeenth century saints.

Beecher never spoke more truly than when he said of Calvinism: "There never was a system since the world stood which put upon man such motives to holiness, or which builds batteries which sweep the whole ground of sin with such terrible artillery. As a matter of fact, wherever this system of truth has been embraced it has produced a noble and distinct type of character—a type so clearly marked that secular historians, with no religious bias, have recognized it, and pointed to it as a remarkable illustration of the power of religious training in the formation of character."[17] At the 250th anniversary of this Assembly it was noted: "We claim, then, for our venerable creed, that whatever the world may say of it, it is fitted to be, and according to the testimony of impartial history, has proved itself to be a *character-making* creed."[18]

From the outset of the Assembly these participants saw themselves as unworthy and consequently wanted it known how much they depended on the grace of God from first to last. In the wording of the Solemn League and Covenant, adopted first in Scotland and later introduced on August 17th, 1643 to the Assembly, they expressed their inner longings in these words: "we profess . . . our unfeigned [sincere] desire to be humbled for our

---

[17] *Memorial Volume of the Westminster Assembly, 1647-1897*, ed. by Francis Beattie, Charles Hemphill, and Henry Escott (Richmond, VA: Presbyterian Committee for Publication, 1897), pp. 261-262.
[18] *Memorial Volume*, p. 265.

own sins . . . especially that we have not as we ought valued the inestimable benefit of the gospel; that we have not labored for the purity and power thereof; and that we have not endeavored to receive Christ in our hearts, nor to walk worthy of him in our lives; which are the cause of other sins and transgressions so much abounding amongst us; and our true and unfeigned purpose, desire, and endeavor for ourselves, and all others under our charge . . . to amend our lives, and each one to go before another in the example of a real reformation; that the Lord may turn away his wrath and heavy indignation, and establish these churches and kingdoms in truth and peace."[19]

The genuine piety of the membership of the Assembly is exemplified in a speech by Philip Nye. While urging adoption of the Solemn League and Covenant, he spoke of the fear of the Lord, the humility requisite for their task, and the necessary simplicity of spirit. Nye called for "courage, spirits that are bold and resolute . . . not amazed amidst much stirs . . . wise statesmen, like an experienced seaman, [who] knows the compass of this vessel, and though it heave and toss, and the passengers cry out about him, yet in the midst of its all, he is himself, turning not aside from his work, but steering on his course."[20] As a prototype of the *pathos* and piety of this group. Nye urged:

> I beseech you, let it be seriously considered, if you mean to do any such work in the house of God as this is; if you mean to pluck up what many years ago was planted, or to build up what so long ago was pulled down, and to go through with this work, and not be discouraged, you must beg of the Lord this excellent spirit, this resolute stirring spirit, otherwise you will be outspirited, and both you and your cause slighted and dishonored.[21]

---

[19] Anon., *A History of the Westminster Assembly of Divines* (Philadelphia, 1841), p. 38.
[20] Reid, op. cit., p. 379.
[21] Ibid., p. 380.

Nye also went on immediately to charge: "On the other hand, we must labor for humility, prudence, gentleness, meekness. A man may be very much zealous and resolute, and yet very meek and merciful: Jesus Christ was a Lion and yet a Lamb also."[22] He concluded his exhortation to adopt the Solemn League and Covenant in a fashion indicative of the Assembly's goal:

> Grant unto us also, that when this life is finished, and we gathered to our fathers, there may be a generation out of our loins to stand up in this cause, that his great, and reverend name may be exalted from one generation to another, until he himself shall come, and perfect all with his own wisdom: even so come Lord Jesus, come quickly. Amen.[23]

These were hearts held out sincerely and promptly to serve God, just as aflame with zeal for the Lord and his house as Calvin and other fathers of the faith had been. These were not sterile academicians; they possessed a passionate zeal for the Lord's honor.

At the covenanting service, the following expressions of prayer and worship were evident: Mr. Wilson expounded verses in the Psalms, with Mr. White praying nearly an hour, followed by another hour-long exhortation by Nye. The commissioners raised their hands as in pledging, after each clause of the Covenant was read. This was followed by another prayer by Dr. Gouge, finalized by adjournment to observe the fast.[24]

Another historian commented on another characteristic of the spirituality of the divines in terms of:

> . . . the sense of humble dependence on God, as seen in the prominence given to prayer. Not only were the daily sessions opened and closed with prayer, and often interspersed with prayer for specific objects, but once a month all business was

---

[22] Ibid., p. 380.
[23] Ibid., p. 381.
[24] Summarized from Beveridge [1904], p. 47.

regularly suspended, that a day of fasting and prayer might be observed in concert with the two houses of Parliament. And what days they were! We read, for instance, in Lightfoot's Journal, that on Friday, October 13, 1643, the order is taken for the fast on the following Monday in these words: 'The time to be from nine to four; the exercises to be the word and prayer, three to pray and two to preach. Dr. Burgess, Mr. Goodwin, and Dr. Stanton to pray, and Mr. Palmer and Mr. Whittacre to preach."[25]

Fasting

A frequent staple of spiritual rejuvenation for the Assembly was the fast. While in the heat of the debate on the form of government, this Assembly was neither oblivious to prayer concerns nor unmindful of the prayers of the saints poured out on the altar. On May 17, 1644, the Assembly adjourned this controversy to fast and pray for the needs of the nation and the army. According to Baillie, the "sweetest day ever seen in England" saw the divines begin a day of prayer with Dr. Twisse leading, followed by two hours of prayers by Mr. Marshall, confessing the sins of the Assembly in a passionate yet prudent manner. Two hours! The fast continued with preaching by John Arrowsmith, succeeded by another two hour prayer time led by by Mr. Vines. Another sermon was offered, and yet another season of prayer was led by Mr. Seaman. This particular fast moved Baillie to say, "God was so evidently in all this exercise, that we expect certainly a blessing both in our matter . . . and in the whole kingdom."[26]

Immediately prior to collecting the Scripture proofs, the Assembly felt an ominous pressure from Parliament. When asked to present their final versions with Scripture references, the Assembly hastily "appointed a day of fasting and humiliation for themselves . . . The fast was observed within their own walls on the 6th of May."[27] This Assembly did not trust in their own

---

[25] *Memorial Volume*, pp. 82-83.
[26] Beveridge [1904], pp. 81-82.
[27] Anon., *A History of the Westminster Assembly of Divines* (Philadelphia,

strength. Rather, they frequently resorted to prayer and fasting. The Scottish ambassadors, keenly aware of the impending storm in England, were "deeply sensible of their own defects . . . [and] the first thing which they did after returning home was to hold a solemn fast to lament their own defection from the solemn league and covenant."[28]

On one occasion, Henry Hall led a solemn fast just prior to the convening of the Assembly (May 29, 1643). On that opportunity he preached on suffering, difficult though it be, as an aid to sanctification. Said Hall, "A Christian is never so glorious, as when he suffers most reproach and ignominy for Christ's sake . . . keep alive this sacred fire, upon the altar of our hearts, that it may inflame our devotion toward God, kindle our love toward men, and burn out all our corruptions."[29]

An early historian said:

> We often find this Assembly engaging in the self-denying duty of fasting; and once a month regularly, they united with the Parliament in observing a solemn fast. On these occasions, nearly the whole day was spent in the public exercises of religion. It is noted by Baillie, that on these solemn occasions, one minister would sometimes pray, without ceasing, for two whole hours. The godly men of that day seem to have been mighty in prayer, and to have known what it was to pray without fainting. Their preaching too, we have reason to believe, from the specimens which have come down to us, was solemn, searching, evangelical, pungent, and powerful. Mr. Baillie incidentally observes, in one of his letters, that Mr. Marshall was reckoned to be the best preacher, and Mr. Palmer the best catechist, in England.[30]

Most of the sermons preached before the Parliament on these fast days were printed later.

Furthermore, the very *Directory for Worship* produced by this

---

1841), p. 124.
[28] Ibid., p. 165.
[29] Reid, Vol. II, p. 6.
[30] Anon., *A History of the Westminster Assembly of Divines* (Philadelphia, 1841), 177-78.

Assembly included separate chapters on fasting and thanksgiving, so important were they as spiritual basics. The original drafts of these were drawn up by the pious Goodwin (fasting) and the moderator, Herle (thanksgiving). Samuel Carruthers described one fast:

> The first of these [fasts] was Monday, 25 September, the day when the Commons and the Divines took the Covenant; they met in St. Margaret's Church, White leading in prayer, Nye speaking a word of exhortation, and Gouge concluding with prayer. Three weeks later (16 October) there was again a day of fasting and prayer, this time in their usual meeting place. It was from nine till four, and during these seven hours (probably not actually continuous) three men (Burges, Goodwin, and Staunton) prayed, and two (Palmer and Whitaker) preached. Lightfoot records that Burges' prayer took an hour, as did also Staunton's. There were four intervals of psalm-singing, but it is not recorded that Scripture was read; and Twisse concluded with prayer. There was a collection (£3 15s.) for maimed soldiers; but next day it was voted to be given to Mrs. Rood, widow of a minister, in straitened circumstances.[31]

The leading historian in the early twentieth century of the Assembly noted:

> On 14 May, 1644, the Lord General, Essex, informed the Divines that he had appointed a fast for the army to be held three days later, and asked them to appoint preachers. They resolved, also at his request, to keep that day as an Assembly fast. Accordingly, Twisse opened with a brief prayer. Then, after singing part of Psalm xxvii, Marshall said, 'Let me speak a few words.' He declared that the nation 'had not had so troublous times for many hundred years;' reminded them that they had been preserved in safety, and that upon them 'the eyes, not only of the kingdom, but of all the churches in Christendom' were fixed. They had expected that much would have been done by

---

[31] Samuel Carruthers, *The Everyday Work of the Westminster Assembly* (London: Presbyterian Historical Society, 1943), p. 65.

now; but 'for some cause or other it pleaseth God that we have had many a sad breach that we cannot drive on so cheerfully.' That was reason enough for humiliation; let each one look into his own heart and see whether he were to blame. Then there was 'common and almost general apostasy in the kingdom;' had they done enough about that? If they did some heart-searching, then, said he, 'we shall find more fruit of one day's musing than of many days' disputing.' He then led in prayer 'for two hours, most divinely, confessing the sins of the members of Assembly in a wonderfully pathetic and prudent way.'[32]

At one fast John Arrowsmith preached for an hour from Haggai 2:4-5, and Richard Vines led in prayer for nearly two hours, followed by a second sermon that also lasted an hour. Samuel Carruthers' details are worth hearing again to capture partially some of the three century old Westminster spirituality.

> On 30 June, 1645, the Commons asked the Divines to make the next day a day of prayer. There was no session of the Assembly the next day. Once more ten churches were named, the occasion being made a public one. On 26 September, 1645, the Divines once more resolved to have a day of humiliation for themselves. This was prompted more by the condition of their own business than by that of public affairs. They appointed Wednesday, 1 October, from 9 a.m. to 4 p.m., and appointed two members 'for exhortation' and three 'for prayer.'[33]

The scope and manner of keeping these fasts is also interesting. "In addition to the regular monthly fast, established by Parliament before the Assembly met, special fasts and thanksgivings were held. The suggestion for these came some-times from Parliament and sometimes from the Assembly; they were sometimes country-wide (so far at least as the authority of the Parliament might at the time extend), usually a week or more later in the provinces than in London, to allow the instructions to be forwarded; at other times

---

[32] Ibid., pp. 65-66.
[33] Ibid., pp. 69-70.

only in certain districts or in certain churches." For example, "[o]n 18 July, 1643, the Assembly suggested a fast 'for the two late disasters in the North and in the West,' but the next day, before they communicated with the Houses, they were informed that one had been fixed for the 21st, and certain divines were asked to preach."[34]

If critics of the Assembly knew more about the prayer lives and fasting of these divines, most criticisms might be delayed until critics exceed the divines' godliness in these areas of spirituality.

Spiritual Battle

In one letter, these divines disclosed their hearts' passion in terms of spiritual warfare: "We doubt not, but the sad reports of the miseries under which the church and kingdom of England do bleed, and wherewith we are ready to be swallowed up, is long since come to your ears; and it is probable, the same instruments of Satan and Antichrist have, by their emissaries, endeavored to present us as black as may be among yourselves."[35]

Their cognizance of the Satanic and the presence of antichristian opposition is apparent from a portion of a letter to Belgic, French, and Swiss churches at the time. The authors' spirituality is seen when they say,

> But though we hoped through the goodness of God, and his blessing . . . that our winter had been past, yet alas! we find it to be quite otherwise. We know our sins have deserved all, and if we die and perish, the Lord is righteous; to his hand we submit, and to him alone we look for healing. The same antichristian faction not being discouraged, by their want of success in Scotland, have stirred up a bloody rebellion in Ireland, wherein above one hundred thousand Protestants have been destroyed in one province . . .[36]

---

[34] Ibid., p. 73.
[35] Anon., *A History of the Westminster Assembly of Divines* (Philadelphia, 1841), p. 54.

This was an Assembly not only of pious men but one acquainted with persecution, loss, and the peril of death. They concluded this appeal by importunately craving,

> your fervent prayers, both public and private, that God would bring salvation to us; that the blessings of truth and peace may rest upon us; that these three nations may be joined as one stick in the hands of the Lord, and that we ourselves, contemptible builders, called to repair the house of God . . . may see the pattern of this house, and commend such a platform of Zerubbabels as may . . . establish uniformity among ourselves; that all mountains may become plains before them and us; that then all who now see the plummet in our hands, may also behold the top-stone set upon the head of the Lord's house among us, and may help us with shouting to cry Grace, grace, to it.[37]

It had also become the practice of the ministers to meet together every Monday to consult together how they might best promote the spread of the gospel. One historian noted that so widespread was the dispersion of piety, that even the military was effected with the result that, "never was an army in which religious feeling, of one kind or another, so predominated. Frequently their commanding officers preached and prayed in public, and the soldiers were deeply imbued with the same spirit, and spent much of their time, when in quarters, in disputing, or praying."[38] This spirit endowed them with invincible courage and admirable piety.

Preaching and Suffering

Experiential Christianity was a forté of these divines. It almost appears that in some way there was a connection between their suffering and their passionate preaching. For example, one unsympathetic poet described Assembly member Edmund Calamy's

---

[36] Ibid., p. 56.
[37] Ibid., p. 58.
[38] Ibid., p. 143.

imprisonment for the faith at Newgate and his preaching style as follows:

> Dead, and yet preach! these Presbyterian slaves
> Will not give over preaching in their graves . . . .
> What can't you Nonconformists be content
> Sermons to make, except you preach them too?[39]

Thus, according to opponents, it was one thing for the Westminster men to believe, but critics detested their spreading the tidings even in jail.

Samuel Rutherford, a participant of the Assembly and author of *Lex Rex*, put it well: "The preaching of the word only, if alone without the Spirit, can no more make an hair white or black, or draw us to the Son, or work repentance in sinners, than the sword of the Magistrate can work repentance. . . . What can preaching of man or angel do without God; is it not God and God only who can open the heart?"[40] This same Rutherford, when preaching on Matthew 9:27-31, proclaimed: "As you have need of Christ in your poverty, by faith you accept of him as a Surety to pay your debts when you are broken and cannot pay them yourselves."[41]

Robert Harris was a divine who was familiar with the pulpit axiom: "I preach, as if I ne'er should preach again; And, as a dying man, to dying men." This same Harris, both a pastor and the President of Trinity College, Oxford, was known for excellent order in nurturing his own children in the faith. In his last will, he stated: "Also, I bequeath to all my children and their children's children, to each of them a Bible with this inscription, *None but Christ*."[42]

His illnesses were public knowledge, and yet he found sweet delight in the Lord accounting as his best days those in which he

---

[39] Reid, pp. 182-183.
[40] Samuel Rutherford, *A Free Disputation . . .*, p. 351 as cited in Warfield, *The Westminster Assembly and Its Work* (rpr. Edmonton: Still Waters Revival Books, 1992), p. 221.
[41] Samuel Rutherford, *The Power of Faith and Prayer* (1713 rpr. Isle of Lewis: Reformation Press, 1991), p. 51
[42] Reid, Vol. II, op. cit., 21.

"enjoyed most intercourse with Heaven." After a long testimony to the power of the fellowship of sufferings with Christ, James Reid commented that Harris "did not expect much from any man, were his parts ever so great, until he was broken by afflictions and temptations."[43] Harris observed with a keen spiritual eye, "[t]hat it was just for God to deny us the comforts of our graces, when we deny him the glory of them," and "[t]hat the humblest preachers converted the greatest number of souls, not the most choice scholars while unbroken."[44] Harris had the insight to say, "[t]hat a preacher has three books to study: the Bible, himself, and the people . . . [and] that preaching to the people was but one part of the pastor's duty: he was to live and die in them, as well as for them."[45] In sickness he said, "I never in all my life saw the worth of Christ, nor tasted the sweetness of God's love, in so great a measure as I now do."

The lesson has been well stated: "The heroism of these great men was sublime, their self-abnegation, Christ-like. Not for glory did they brave death, not for honors did they toil, but because they were constrained by the love of Christ and of their fellow-men. I would that you, my spiritual fathers, would read more of these 'living epistles' to your people from your pulpits."[46]

Matthew Newcomen, one of the divines, spoke of preaching as "the greater light of heaven," when he charged the Assembly at its outset to have courage:

> Keep no silence, give the Lord no rest until He establish the house . . . except the Lord build the house, reform the Church, it is to no purpose to go about to reform it. . . . I need not tell you how many eyes and expectations there are upon this Assembly. . . . . what you pray for, contend for: . . . as you pray that God would establish his Church in peace, so labor to work out the Church's peace. And lastly, as you pray that God would make

---

[43] Ibid., p. 23.
[44] Ibid., 23.
[45] Idem.
[46] *Anniversary Addresses,* p. 40.

the Church a praise, so endeavor that also; endeavoring . . . that all her ways may be ordered according to the rule of God's Word: that the Gospel may run and be glorified: that those two great illuminating ordinances of Preaching and Catechizing, which are as the greater and lesser lights of heaven, may have such liberty, encouragement, maintenance, that all the earth may be filled with the knowledge of the Lord.[47]

Many have estimated that the Puritan preaching of the 1640s was among the most influential in history. During that decade, over 240 sermons (185 of which were on OT texts and very few were from the Pauline Epistles[48]) were preached to Parliament, and "[e]very facet of individual and social life was informed and under-stood by a faith that was subject to Scripture."[49] Rather than utilizing modern features of pulpit ministry such as attempts at humor, levity, drama, and entertainment, these Puritans knew the power of the pulpit to be the dominant medium. Robert Norris reminds us that:

> Any philosophy of preaching that forgets the gravity of the task and neglects the lessons of Westminster will forgo the powerful effects produced by the preaching of those times. We will not serve the present generation by neglecting the lessons of the past. And while sacred eloquence assumes different forms in different generations, and while no time or church can claim perfection in the manner of presenting the truth, rarely has any one Christian assembly produced better counsel backed with the testimony of proven result than the divines assembled at Westminster.[50]

Another glimpse into the Westminster divines' use of the pulpit for spiritual formation may be seen in a typical (and excellent) ongoing series of "exhortations." A decade after the adjournment

---

[47] Cited in *Journal of Presbyterian History*, vol. xxi, nos. 2 and 3, pp. 126-127.
[48] Cf. Robert M. Norris, "The Preaching of the Assembly," *To Glorify and Enjoy God: A Commemoration of the Westminster Assembly*, John L. Carson and David W. Hall, eds. (Edinburgh: Banner of Truth Trust, 1994), pp. 65, 73.
[49] Ibid., p. 66.
[50] Ibid., p. 81.

of the Assembly, several of the divines united to give sermons at "The Morning Exercises at Cripplegate, St. Giles in the Fields, and in Southwark." These exhortations or practical sermons were given by the presbyters near London, many of whom had been supportive of the aims of the Assembly. Even if all of the "Morning Exercise" preachers were not actually involved in the Assembly, there is no evidence that they differed with the *ethos* of the Assembly. A glance at their topics illumines the practical emphasis on spirituality, as well as the priority of preaching. A sample of the sermons (from Westminster divines) below highlights the spiritual thrust of the preaching:

- "What Must and Can Persons do Toward Their Own Conversion?" (Ez. 18:32) by William Greenhill;
- "Now is the Time: Or, Instructions for the Present improving the Season of Grace" (2 Cor. 6:1-2) by William Jenkin;
- "On Sabbath Sanctification" (Is. 63:13-14) by Thomas Case;
- "How Ought We to Bewail the Sins of the Places where we Live?" (2 Pet. 2:7-8) by William Jenkin.[51]

Confession of Sins

As noted above, these divines were not afraid to confess their sins. On one occasion "Palmer rose with the words, 'I desire to begin there,' and opened with the fault of slack attendance, coming late and going early, especially the sparse attendance at committees. It throws a curious light upon their proceedings that he said that during the meetings there was 'reading of news,' 'talking and in confusion; we do not attend at the beginning nor ending for prayer as we ought to do.' His next complaint is also a perennial one: 'On the one hand,

---

[51] Taken from *Puritan Sermons, 1659-1689*, (Wheaton, IL: Richard Owen Roberts, 1981), vols. 1-6. Many other sermons and "cases of conscience" were addressed by the likes of John Owen, Thomas Manton, Robert Trail, Thomas Watson, Richard Baxter, and Stephen Charnock at these preaching sessions.

some of us are too forward to speak, and some are, I fear too backward.' Finally, he referred to 'unhappy differences and unbeseeming phrases.'"[52]

Charles Herle was not afraid to admit the sins of the Assembly publicly and arranged a list of offenses of the Assembly in order to expedite confession (below):

I. *The sins of the Assembly*. 1. Neglect of the service, in slackness in coming and departing at pleasure; 2. By abstaining from prayers; 3. Manifesting a neglect in the time of debate, and neglecting committees; 4. Some speaking too much, and others too little; 5. By irreverent carriage; 6. By haste in debating; 7. Driving on parties; 8. Not serious examination of ministers.

II. *Of the armies*. 1. Emulation among the officers, causing the loss of many opportunities; 2. Want of ministers; 3. Swearing, drinking, etc., 4. Want of discipline in the army.

III. *Of the people*. 1. Profaneness, scorn of God's hand upon us; 2. Duties of humiliation 'disfigured'; 3. Our hearts not humbled upon humiliation; there was 'curling of hair, patching, bare breasts, and painting'; 4. Divisions in opinion and affection among professors; 5. Jealousies, sidings, and tale-bearings; 6. Unthankfulness for God's mercies; 7. Neglect of personal and family reformation; 8. Carnal confidence and general security.

IV. *Of Parliament*. 1. Not tendering the Covenant to all in their power; 2. Not active in suppressing Anabaptists and Antinomians; 3. Not seeking religion in the first place; 4. Not suppressing state plays, taverns, profaneness, and scoffing of ministers, and even incest itself; 5. Not a free publishing of truths, for fear of losing a party; 6. Oppression

---

[52] Carruthers, op. cit., p. 76.

by committees, with intolerable fees; 7. Not debts paid; 8. Remissness in punishing delinquents; 9. Private ends aimed at, 'the great incomes of some new invented offices'; 10. Delays in relieving the army; 11. Church lands sold, but not for the maintenance of ministers.[53]

Spiritual Formation of the Family

Another aspect of spirituality was the undying commitment of these Assembly-men to the spiritual nurture of children, the family, the sabbath, and character formation. As observed at the 250th anniversary of the Westminster Assembly:

> There is a most real and vital connection between belief and conduct, between creed and character. What men believe, that they become. As Bacon says: 'Truth and goodness differ but as the seal and the print; for truth prints goodness.' The same may be said of error and evil. Evil in conduct and character is ever the imprint of error. . . . Today we are to inquire how the Standards, framed by the Westminster Assembly, abide this test. How have they stood translation into real life or incarnation in living men and women? Have their practical effects been such as to vindicate their right to survive among the creeds of Christendom? What influence have they exerted upon 'the individual, the family, and society,' where they have been embraced? . . . The Westminster divines well understood the necessity of training up a child in the way he should go in order to insure against his departing from it in age. They heard and heeded the risen Master's commission to Simon Peter, 'Feed my *lambs.*' Their very best work, in the judgment of many, is found in the provision which they made for the lambs of the flock. Richard Baxter is quoted as saying: 'If the Westminster Assembly had done nothing more than produce the Shorter Catechism they would be entitled to the everlasting gratitude of the Christian church.' He further expressed the opinion that, next to the Bible, it was probably the best book in the world. Hence, wherever these doctrines have been received they have brought

---

[53] Ibid., p. 80.

forth the fruits of righteousness. What Dr. Chalmers said of Scotland is true the world over: 'Wherever there has been most Calvinism, men have been most moral.'[54]

The beliefs and the practiced spirituality were two sides of the same coin for the Westminster fathers. The "character developed among them was as pure and noble as it was distinct. It is safe to say it has seldom been surpassed in the history of the world. That they had their faults goes without saying. But even their 'failings,' as Burns said of his father's, were such as 'leaned to virtue's side.'"[55]

One of the tell-tale emblems of Westminster spirituality was the honoring and loving of God on a regular, sabbatical basis. Scottish commissioner to the Westminster Assembly, Archibald Johnston, exemplified the spiritual thrust of the Sabbath as he prayed in 1655: "O Lord Jesus, woo Thou their hearts, warme their affections, revive their spirits, gayne their loves; let it be as a resurrection from the dead."[56] On another fast-day,[57] Johnston recorded, "I got several tymes teares in the church prayers, and between sermons with my wyfe, and then in privat with great freedom."[58] The pitch of spirituality is seen in this prayer and memoir by Lord Wariston: "O Lord, speak graciously to the remnant, and cause our ears to hear Thee. Oh, I feared our abusing the Lord's patience, who has restrayned the rod now from overflowing . . . and has delayed His anger to see if wee would repent and returne."[59] Historian William H. Roberts,

---

[54] *Memorial Volume*, pp. 257-258, 260.
[55] *Memorial Volume*, p. 262.
[56] *The Diary of Sir Archibald Johnston of Wariston* (Edinburgh: Scottish Historical Society, 1940) Third Series, vol. XXXIV, p. 9.
[57] Johnston frequently refers to fasts (*The Diary of Sir Archibald Johnston of Wariston* (Edinburgh: Scottish Historical Society, 1919) Second Series, vol. XVIII, pp. 139, 302, 303) and the Lord's Day (Ibid., pp. 43, 130, 303).
[58] *The Diary of Sir Archibald Johnston of Wariston* (Edinburgh: Scottish Historical Society, 1919) Second Series, vol. XVIII, p. 16.
[59] *The Diary of Sir Archibald Johnston of Wariston* (Edinburgh: Scottish Historical Society, 1919) Second Series, vol. XVIII, p. 56.

commemorating the spiritual disciplines of the divines a hundred years ago, made this correlation:

> The family and the Sabbath! The two institutions of Eden which survived the wreck of the fall! They are the two strong supports of all social order, the Jachin and Boaz upon which human society rests. Let them be disintegrated and social chaos inevitably follows. These two institutions our venerable Standards exalt as no others do. For their maintenance the Presbyterian Church has always stood. . . . they have been handed down to us as a precious legacy from God-fearing ancestors . . . a high trust, to be passed on in unimpaired integrity to generations yet to come. . . . These two springs of blessing have been opened for us, at unspeakable cost, by hearts and hands long stilled in death. We have drunk from them and been refreshed. . . . There are no institutions of our holy religion which the great enemy of all good is attacking today with more persistent or subtle malignity and zeal.[60]

We also observe the great emphasis on the family as a primary sphere in which the Westminster faith was propagated. One fruit of Westminster is its influence on discipling the family. The role of the family as the chief propagator of the faith can be seen by the extensive use among Westminster adherents of catechism for instructing the young. The Westminster tradition placed a premium on godly parents instructing their covenant children in the principles of the true religion through the catechism. Moreover, family devotionals were a staple for the piety of the Westminster Assembly and great use of family nurture was evident. These made the most of the proverb: "As the twig is bent, the tree is inclined."[61]

On the value of the catechisms and early memorization, a century ago the potential for the influence of the Catechism on youth was estimated as follows:

> 1. Unless they are learned in childhood and youth, the strong

---

[60] *Memorial Volume*, pp. 268-269.
[61] *Anniversary Addresses*, p. 230.

probability is that they will never be learned at all. Not one in five hundred of our people, perhaps, learns them later in life. They must be learned, then, early in life, or never. Are we willing for the latter alternative? Are we willing that our children shall never *accurately* know the great truths of religion? Are we willing that they shall never accurately know what is meant by such doctrines as faith, and repentance, and justification, and sanctification? Would that be wise? Would that be safe?

2. We cannot too early impress the great truths of the Catechisms on their minds and hearts . . . in childhood and youth the soul is most susceptible of deep and lasting impressions. In our great museums we sometimes see stone slabs with the marks of raindrops on them that fell before man had any existence, and the impressions of the feet of tiny birds. . . . So, in childhood and youth, the souls of our children are most susceptible of impressions for good or evil; and then, as the years elapse, those souls, with those impressions on them, indurate; and thus those impressions become as lasting, as everlasting, it may be, as the souls themselves. How important it is, then, that these earliest and most enduring impressions should be made in behalf of right and truth and God by the inculcation of the great truths of our Catechisms!

3. It is necessary to our success as a denomination that our Catechisms be intelligently and faithfully taught. Our doctrines are constantly and bitterly assailed. In much of the literature of the day, especially in that kind which, unfortunately, our children too much read, they are caricatured as severe, harsh, unreasonable, antiquated; as belonging to a remote and ignorant past; as being entirely out of harmony with the progress that has been made in better views of the benevolence, of the divine nature, of the dignity of man, and of the vastness and freeness of redeeming love.[62]

A document written contemporaneous with the drafting of the Westminster Confession also exhibits the strong views of the

---

[62] *Memorial Volume,* pp. 136-137.

family held by the Scottish commissioners. In 1647, the Scottish General Assembly approved a *Directory for Family Worship*. This document reflected the views as well as the sentiments of many of the members of the Westminster Assembly on the importance of family worship. So essential was family worship—not only as a supplement to regular worship on the Lord's Day—that the Scottish presbyters laid out directions that were to be used to augment building up of faith, cherishing piety, maintaining of unity, and deterring schism among godly families. So important was this family faith that the Scottish General Assembly even called upon presbyteries to require those within their bounds to carry these things out at the threat of discipline and moreover that every individual family was to practice family worship. "And if any such family be found, the head of the family is to be first admonished privately to amend his fault; and, in case of his continuing therein, he is to be gravely and sadly reproved by the session; after which reproof, if he be found still to neglect Family-worship, let him be, for his obstinacy in such an offence, suspended and debarred from the Lord's supper, as being justly esteemed unworthy to communicate therein, till he amend."

Missionary Zeal

Another mistake of those who are not thoroughly familiar with the Westminster divines is to allege that they had little or no interest in foreign missions. As early as John Calvin there was interest in evangelizing the Villegagnon Colony (Brazil).[63] By 1641, fifteen divines who would become commissioners to the Westminster Assembly joined William Castell in a petition calling for the evangelization of the New World. In addition to these, two of the Scottish divines, Alexander Henderson and Robert Baillie, joined their names to the petition that had seventy signatories. The petition began with a lament about "the great and general neglect of this

---

[63] "The Westminster Divines and Foreign Missions," *Journal of the Presbyterian Histor-ical Society*, vol. xxi, June and September, 1943, nos. 2 and 3, p. 148.

kingdome, in not propagating the glorious Gospel in America, a maine part of the world."[64] The petition continued:

> Although some of the reformed religion, English, Scotch, French, and Dutch, have already taken up their habitations in those parts, yet both their going thither (as yet) has been to small purpose, for the converting of those nations, either for that they have placed themselves but in the skirts of America, where there are but few natives (as those in New England), or else for want of able and conscionable ministers (as in Virginia) they themselves are become exceeding rude, more likely to turn Heathen, than to turn others to the Christian faith.[65]

The petitioners noted that "there is no great difficulty in the preparation here, or tediousnesse in the passage thither, or hazard when wee come there. . . . It being ordinarily by six weeks sayle, in a sea much more secure for Pirats . . . And as for our good successe there, wee need not fear it. The natives being now everywhere more than ever, out of an inveterate hatred to the Spaniard, ready and glad to entertained us."[66]

Signed by Westminster divines R. Brownricke, R. Sanderson, D. Featly, M. Styles, E. Stanton, G. Walker, J. Caryl, E. Calamy, A. Byfield, W. Price, J. White, H. Paynter, S. Marshall, J. Burroughes, and J. Whittaker, this petition to Parliament concluded:

> And which is much more our going with a generall consent in Gods cause, for the promoting of the Gospel, and inlarging of his church, may assure us of a more than ordinary protection and direction. That hitherto, wee have been lesse successfull in our voyage that way, wee may justly impute it to this, that as yet they have not beene undertaken with such a generall consent, and with such a full reference to Gods glory as was requisite. And so your Petitioner having delivered his apprehension herein,

---

[64] Idem.
[65] Ibid., p. 149.
[66] Ibid., p. 156.

more briefly, then so weighty a matter might well require, he submits all the premises to your more full deliberation and conclusion, which hee humbly prayeth, may bee with all convenient speed; the onely best way under God to make it the better successfull . . . concerning the propagation of the glorious Gospel of Christ in America.[67]

The Scottish Parliament also received a similar bill, signed by Henderson and Baillie:

The motion made by Master William Castell, Minister of the Gospel, for propagating of the blessed Evangell of Christ our Lord and Savior in America, wee conceive in the generall to bee most pious, Christian and charitable. And therefore worthy to be seriously considered, of all that love the glorious name of Christ, and are zealous of the salvation of soules, which are without Christ, and without God in the world, wishing the opportunity and fit season: the instruments and means. And all things necessary for the prosecution of so pious a worke, to bee considered by the wisedomes of Churches and civil powers, whom God hath called, and enables with Piety, Prudence, and Peace, for matters of publicke concernment, and of so great Importance, And beseeching the Lord to blesse all their consultations and proceedings for the advancing and establishing the Kingdome of Jesus Christ.[68]

In addition, the work of John Eliot to the American missionaries illustrates that these divines were neither narrow in their concerns nor sterile in their spiritual impulses. About the time of the conclusion of the Assembly, the following pamphlets were published in London: *The Day-Breaking, if not the Sun-rising of the Gospel with the Indians in New-England* (1647); *The Clear Sun-shine of the Gospel, etc.* (1648); *The Glorious Progress of the Gospel, etc.* (1649); *The Light appearing more and more towards the perfect Day, etc.* (1651); *Strength out of Weaknesse* (1652); and

---

[67] Ibid., p. 157.
[68] Ibid., pp. 158-159.

Tears of Repentance (1653). These demonstrate a devout concern for missions.

Scripture

No survey of Westminster spirituality would be complete without reference to the admiration of the divines for Scripture, which they viewed as both the authority for life and a devotional staple. The Assembly was so emphatically tied to the Bible that they even proposed a study Bible. A committee was commissioned to make "[t]he Annotations of the Westminster Assembly." Annotations to the Pentateuch, the OT historical books, Psalms, Proverbs, the major prophets, the Gospels, and Paul's Epistles were compiled. However, these were never published with the sanction of Parliament.

On the views of Assembly members and the Bible, Calamy, one of the most astute professors also commented,

> There are two great Gifts that God hath given to his people. The *Word Christ*, and the *Word of Christ*; Both are unspeakably great; but the first will do us no good without the second. . . . Blessed be God who hath not only given us the book of the Creatures, and the book of Nature to know himself and his will by; but also, and especially the book of Scriptures, whereby we come to know those things of God, and of Christ, which neither the book of Nature nor of the Creatures can reveal unto us. Let us bless God, not only for revealing his Will in his Word, but for revealing it by writing.[69]

One of the participants of the Assembly, Anthony Burgess, wrote in another place on this same topic: "As for that dangerous opinion, that makes God's calling of man to repentance by the Creatures, to be enough and sufficient, we reject, as that which cuts at the very root of free grace: A voice, indeed, we grant they have, but yet they make Paul's trumpet, an uncertain sound; men cannot by them [creational revelation] know the nature of God and his Worship, and wherein our Justification doth consist."[70]

---

[69] Edward Calamy, *The Godly Man's Ark*. London, 1672, pp. 55-56, and 90 as cited in Warfield, *The Westminster Assembly and Its Work,* p. 198.

John Arrowsmith, another member of the Assembly and one of the leading theological professors of the time, said similarly, "For to maintain (as some do) that a man may be saved in an ordinary course . . . by any religion whatsoever, provided he live according to the principles of it, is to turn the whole world into an Eden; and to find a Tree of Life in every garden, as well as in the paradise of God."[71]

Even more to the point, Assembly member William Bridge stated, "Though Human Reason be a Beam of Divine Wisdom, yet if it be not enlightened with an higher Light of the Gospel, it cannot reach unto the things of God as it should. . . . For though reason be the Gift of God, yet it doth proceed from God as he is God, and General Ruler of the World."[72]

The Scotsman George Gillespie wrote: "The Scripture is known to be indeed the word of God by the beams of divine authority it hath in itself . . . such as the heavenliness of the matter; the majesty of the style; the irresistible power over the conscience; the general scope, to abase man and to exalt God; nothing driven at but God's glory and man's salvation . . . the supernatural mysteries revealed therein, which could never have entered the reason of men; the marvelous consent of all parts and passages (though written by divers and several penmen), even where there is some appearance of difference . . . these, and the like, are characters and marks which evidence the Scriptures to be the word of God."[73]

Calamy attested,

> It is certain that all Scripture is of Divine inspiration, and that the holy men of God spake as they were guided by the Holy Ghost. . . . It transcribes the mind and heart of God. A true Saint loveth

---

[70] Anthony Burgess in *Spiritual Refining,* London, 1652, p. 588 as cited in Warfield *supra,* p. 197.
[71] John Arrowsmith in *A Chain of Principles,* Cambridge, 1659, p. 128 as cited in Warfield *supra,* pp. 197-198.
[72] William Bridge, *Scripture-Light, the Most Sure Light,* London, 1656, pp. 32-33, as cited in Warfield, p. 199.
[73] Cf. Gillespie's *Miscellaneous Questions,* p. 105-106 of the Presbyterian's Armory edition, cited by Warfield, p. 176.

the Name, Authority, Power, Wisdom, and Goodness of God in every letter of it, and therefore cannot but take pleasure in it. It is an Epistle sent down to him from the God of heaven . . . The Word of God hath God for its Author, and therefore must needs be full of Infinite Wisdom and Eloquence, even the Wisdom and Eloquence of God. There is not a word in it, but breathes out God, and is breathed out by God. It is . . . an invariable rule of Faith, an *unerring* (emphasis added) and infallible guide to heaven.[74]

All the Scriptures are *theopneustoi* ["God-breathed" as in 2 Tim. 3:16] by Divine inspiration; and therefore the breathings of God's spirit, are to be expected in this Garden: and those commands of attending to the Scripture only, and to observe what is written, is a plain demonstration that God hath tied us to the Scriptures only: so that as the child in the womb liveth upon nourishment conveyed by the Navel cleaving to it, so doth the Church live only upon Christ by the Navel of the scripture, through which all nourishment is conveyed.[75]

Of the autographs as the authority and without error, Daniel Featly said, "If you will dispute in Divinity, you must be able to produce the Scriptures in the Original Languages. For no Translation is simply Authentical, or the undoubted word of God. In the undoubted word of God there can be no error. But in Translations there may be, and are errors. The Bible translated therefore is not the undoubted Word of God, but so far only as it agreeth with the Original."[76]

Edward Reynolds wrote, "The scriptures . . . are the alone rule of all controversies . . . So then the only light by which differences are to be decided, is the word, being a full canon of God's revealed will."[77] Samuel Rutherford was of the opinion that, "The Scripture makes it self the judge and determiner of all questions and

---

[74] *The Godly Man's Ark,* pp. 55, 80 as cited in Warfield, pp. 208-209.
[75] Anthony Burgess in *Spiritual Refining,* p. 152 as cited in Warfield, p. 208.
[76] Cited by Warfield, p. 242.
[77] *Works,* v., pp. 152-153, 1826 as cited in Warfield, p. 256.

DIVINE CHARACTER

controversies in religion."[78] Youthful George Gillespie spoke of "the written word of God [as] surer than any voice which can speak in the soul of a man, and an inward testimony may sooner deceive us than the written word can; which being so, we may and ought to try the voice which speaks in the soul by the voice of the Lord which speaks in the Scripture."[79]

The leading scholar at the Assembly of the Bible in its original languages, John Lightfoot, clarified the importance of the Scripture this way: "How may Christians inquire of God in their doubtings, as Israel did . . . in theirs? I answer briefly, . . . to the written word of God, Search the Scriptures. . . . There is now no other way to inquire of God, but only from his word."[80]

As to the modern question of whether or not the Westminster Confession of Faith advocated the inerrancy of Scripture, the above citations should be sufficient. Other contemporaries of the Westminster Assembly, such as Richard Baxter, a leading Puritan of the day, uttered the following.

> May one be saved who believeth that the Scripture hath any mistake of error, and believeth it not all? . . . He that thinketh that the prophets, sacred historians, evangelists, and apostles, were guided to an infallible delivery and recording of all the great, substantial, necessary points of the gospel, but not to an infallibility in every by-expression, phrase, citation, or circumstance, doth disadvantage his own faith as to all the rest; but yet may be saved, if he believe the substance with a sound and practical belief.[81]

Samuel Rutherford wrote:

---

[78] *A Free Disputation,* London, 1649, p. 361 as cited in Warfield, p. 256.
[79] *Miscellaneous Questions,* 1649 as cited by Warfield, p. 256.
[80] *Works of John Lightfoot,* vi, p. 286 as cited in Warfield, p. 256.
[81] An excellent summary of these contemporaneous views is set forth in the article, "Inerrancy, Infallibility, and Scripture in the Westminster Confession of Faith" by John Delivuk in the *Westminster Theological Journal,* Fall 1992, vol. 54, no. 2, pp. 349-355.

Whereas the means of conveying the things believed may be fallible, as writing, printing, translating, speaking, are all fallible means of conveying the truth of old and new Testament to us, and yet the Word of God in that which is delivered to us is infallible, 1. For let the Printer be fallible. 2. The translation fallible. 3. The grammar fallible. 4. The man that readeth the word or publisheth it fallible, yet this hindereth not but the truth itself in the written word of God is infallible.[82]

Edward Reynolds, a member of the Assembly, tied the unfailingness of Scripture to the attributes of God. Reynolds wrote:

1. That God in his authority is infallible, who neither can be deceived, nor can deceive. 2. That the things, delivered in holy Scriptures are the dictates and truths, which that infallible authority hath delivered unto the church to be believed; and therefore that every supernatural truth, there plainly set down . . . in an unquestionable principle; and everything, but evident consequence and deduction from thence derived, is therefore an undoubted conclusion in theological and divine knowledge.[83]

Furthermore, Reynolds was clear when he said,

First, That God is of infallible authority, and cannot lie nor deceive: which thing is a principle, . . . And, secondly, That this authority, which in faith I thus rely upon, is, indeed and infallibly, God's own authority. . . . in regard to our weakness and distrust, we are often subject to stagger, yet, in the thing itself, it dependeth upon the infallibility of God's own Word, who hath said it, and is, by consequence, nearer unto Him who is the fountain of all truth; and therefore must need more share in the properties of truth, which are certainty and evidence . . . [84]

John Delivuk concludes,

---

[82] Ibid., p. 352.
[83] Ibid., p. 353.
[84] Ibid., p. 354.

Edward Reynolds and the other authors of the WCF believed that the Bible was inerrant. This was shown above by the seventeenth-century meaning of the word infallible, the confession writers' use of infallible in contexts where it could be used interchangeably with inerrant, and by their view of Scripture as the product of a perfect God, who had given some his attributes, such as truth and perfection, to his word. The combined evidence of these three points leads one to conclude that the authors of the confession believed strongly in the inerrancy of the Bible. . . . The authors of the confession believed that the Bible is reliable and true in all matters which it addresses, that it is completely free from all errors, falsehoods, or deceits, and that this truthfulness extends to all matters religious and secular.[85]

Final Spirituality

A final attribute of this sophisticated spirituality is bravery. "Courage is another trait which to a marked degree has characterized such as are moulded by this creed. . . . He who believes in an Almighty Father, who has foreordained whatsoever comes to pass, and who through his overruling providence is preserving and governing all his creatures, and all their actions, is made superior to those experiences of life which cause others to quake and fear. Hence, Bancroft says, 'A coward and a Puritan never went together.'" [86]

Such bravery is evident in the death-bed testimonies of some of these divines. On dying in a manner worthy of our Lord, Jeremiah Whittaker put it this way:

> O, my God, break open the prison door, and set my poor captive soul free: but enable me to wait willingly thy time. I desire to be dissolved. Never was any man more desirous of life, than I am of death. When will that time come, when I shall neither sin nor

---

[85] Ibid., p. 355. Cf. also John Delivuk, "Some Hermeneutical Principles of the Westminster Confession" in *Evangelical Hermeneutics*, Michael Bauman and David W. Hall, eds. (Camp Hill, PA: Christian Publications, 1995).
[86] *Memorial Volume,* pp. 263-264.

sorrow anymore? When shall mortality put on immortality? . . . The soul that would be truly wise, And taste substantial joys, Must rise above this giddy world, And all its trifling toys. Our treasure and hearts with God, We die to all on earth.[87]

Often the truest measure of Christian vitality is weighed at the conclusion of life. When all was completed, when the fruit was harvested, these divines were some of the most excellent Christians ever, certainly enough to induce us to give a respectful consideration of their words and works. Joseph Caryl was one such member of this Assembly who though dead still speaks. About him, as an example of piety, it was elegized,

> His pious sermons did declare his worth,
> His expositions set his learning forth; . . .
> As in some mirror you might clearly see
> In him, a perfect map of Piety;[88]

Samuel Rutherford was known as an ardent defender of the faith. Flavel commended him for contending against the sectarians of the day, while Robert Baillie extolled Rutherford as a champion against diverse enemies and specifically against the antinomians. Piety was one of his greatest attributes. As he was dying, Rutherford uttered, "I feed upon manna, I have angels' food, my eyes shall see my Redeemer, I know that He shall stand at the latter day on the earth, and I shall be caught up in the clouds to meet Him in the air . . . I sleep in Christ, and when I awake I shall be satisfied with his likeness. O for arms to embrace him."[89] His final words were, "Glory, glory dwells in Emmanuel's land." In the hymn "The Sands of Time are Sinking," Annie Cousins paraphrased the dying words of pious Rutherford, exhibiting the final level of this man's convictions. Perhaps many have sung this hymn without knowing it originated from the sentiments of one of the members of the Westminster Assembly.

---

[87] Reid, Vol. II, pp. 232-234.
[88] Reid, pp. 198-199.
[89] Reid, II, p. 357.

Oh! Christ, he is the fountain,
The deep, sweet well of love;
The streams on earth I've tasted,
I'll drink more deep above.
There to an ocean fullness
His mercy doth expand,
And glory, glory dwelleth
In Immanuel's land.[90]

Conclusion

These lives are full of piety and well worth knowing. They are examples of timeless spirituality, well-rounded, balanced, and stable. Most will be spurred on to greater faithfulness in Christian living by studying the men of Westminster. Reflecting on the value of familiarity with these divines, James Reid noted:

> a brilliant constellation at Westminster... [of] sound principles, Christian dispositions, and conversation becoming the gospel of Christ. In these, we may clearly see the power of divine grace shining forth in all its glory in real life, subduing the inbred corruptions of our fallen nature, and animating to every good word and work. In these, we may see pious and learned men eminently zealous in the advancement of true religion, and earnestly contending for the faith which was once delivered unto the saints.[91]

On the benefit of reviving the influence of this spiritual vitality, one hundred years ago Robert Coyle urged:

> What we need to multiply conversions, to make our preaching mighty, to kindle our missionary fires, to set every Board free from the incubus of debt, to bring us together, North and South,

---

[90] Many other biographical sketches are available to further these and other lessons in spirituality. For a particularly helpful recent work, cf. William S. Barker, *Puritan Profiles* (Geanies House, Fearn, Ross-shire, Scotland: Christian Focus Publications, 1996).

[91] Reid, Vol. II, p. 3.

to unite the entire Presbyterian family, and send us forth upon a new career of conquest and glory, is a revival of loyalty to our King. What is needed is to get away from side issues, away from the catching themes of the hour, away from themes literary, and themes political, and themes social, and themes exploited by the daily press, and lift up the name of our King, and make it pre-eminent above every name. Unless this is done, agnosticism and materialism will win the day. Unless this is done, the pulpit will go into eclipse.[92]

Often overlooked is the fact that these Westminster standards also have influence and potential for unity.

Some do not like creeds; but our Church has always thought it fair and honorable to state explicitly what it understands the Word of God to teach. Our Creed then is our witness-bearer to the whole world. Indeed, no man can write or preach a sermon without stating in part his creed, and we are bound to contend earnestly for the faith once delivered to the saints. At the same time our Creed is pre-eminently an irenical document, and we believe the clear, definite statement by the Christian denominations of what they believe, is the very best road to an ultimate agreement of the churches on the fundamental and essential doctrines of our holy religion.[93]

The examples of these divines are of enduring value and in no way outdated for they represent God's eternal truths. Of existing resources among Christians, these practices are still among the best, although they are frequently ignored. Rather than being so dismissive, we should know something of the inner lives of those divines at Westminster. It helps to know what spiritual disciplines were used by Christians three and a half centuries ago.

Many Christians have already plowed the furrows of spiritual formation. In this discipline, we do not unearth much that is radically new. In the main, we merely dust off a great chapter of history that is not so different from our own times. Since the faith is the same in 1643 as in 1993 (cf. Jude 3), we find some

---

[92] *Anniversary Addresses,* 1898, p. 145. Note, and it did!!
[93] *Anniversary Addresses,* p. 176.

agreement with Chesterton who called the church, a "democracy of the dead," meaning that if we truly understand the unity of the church—both militant and triumphant—we will not want to disenfranchise those in our church who have gone home to be with the Lord. They, too, have much to say in the referenda of today.

Measuring the influence of Westminster by its ability to inspire extraordinary spiritual courage and loyalty, the comment was made a century ago that, "Rather than yield their rights of conscience, 2000 English Presbyterian ministers, on St. Bartholomew's Day, 1662, showed the stuff they were made of by leaving their churches, their support, their homes, their weeping flocks, and becoming strangers and wanderers in their native land. It was this doctrine that put into the Presbyterians of Scotland the strength and stability of their own granite hills. . . . Happy will it be for our denomination if this day shall kindle something more of that spirit in us, and send us to our homes and our people to pass it along."[94]

Nor are these merely past sentiments, true only for an earlier age. At a commemoration of the Assembly one century ago, the record was set straight:

> The accusations which their opponents have made against them have, in most instances, been encomiums. They have been criticized for being too strict and uncompromising in their views of life and duty. But all excellence is marked by strictness. Strictness certainly characterizes everything which truly represents God. The laws of nature are all strict; the laws of hygiene are strict; and the life which would secure their benediction must be a strict life. So with the laws of morals. Like him who ordained them they know 'no variableness nor shadow of turning.' Any pretended exposition of the moral nature and claims of God which is characterized by looseness, by that very tact brands itself as false. Their narrowness has been unctuously deplored. But after all is it not the narrowness of truth? The Master himself said, 'Strait is the gate and narrow is the way which leadeth unto life, and few there be that find it.' 'Narrowness,' it has been said, 'is often the badge of usefulness.' Great leaders of men have been narrow.

---

[94] *Anniversary Addresses,* pp. 140-141.

Elijah was too narrow to adopt the worship of Baal. Martin Luther was too narrow to include in his creed the errors of the Papacy. Wesley was too narrow to sympathize with the cold ritualism of his age. William Carey was so narrow that he had no sympathy with the anti-mission spirit of his age. Gideon was so narrow that he could not tolerate the idols in his father's house, but rose in his might and tore them down. The narrowness of Calvinists has usually been of the same sort.[95]

---

[95] *Memorial Volume,* pp. 262-263.

Bibliography and Sources

PRIMARY SOURCES

Robert Baillie, *The Letters and Journals of Robert Baillie* (3 Vols): https://newbooksinpolitics.com/political/the-letters-and-journals-of-robert-baillie/.

Jeremiah Burroughs, *Gospel-Worship: The Right Manner of Sanctifying the Name of God in General* (Soli Dei Gloria, 1993).

Youngchun Cho, *Anthony Tuckney (1599-1670): Theologian of the Westminster Assembly* (Grand Rapids, MI: Reformation Heritage Books, 2010).

George Gillespie, *Notes of Debates and Proceedings of the Assembly of Divines at Westminster, February 1644 to January 1645* (Still Waters Revival Books, 1991).

George Gillespie, *Against the English Popish Ceremonies* (1637, rpr Dallas, TX, Naphtali Press, 1993).

George Gillespie, *Aaron's Rod Blossoming* (Dallas, TX, Naphtali

Press, 1991).

Ministers of Sion College, *Jus Divinum*, David W. Hall, ed. (Powder Springs, GA, Covenant Foundation, 2018); also an abridged edition of this was published as *The Divine Plan for Church Structure,* Covenant Foundation, 2018).

Alexander Mitchell and John Struthers, ed., *The Minutes of the Sessions of the Westminster Assembly* (1874, rpr. Still Waters Revival Books, 1991).

Chad van Dixhoorn, ed., *The Minutes and Papers of the Westminster Assembly, 1643-1653* [5 vols] (Oxford University Press, 2012).

Westminster Assembly Project website: https://www.westminsterassembly.org/primary-source

HISTORIES

William Beveridge, *A Short History of the Westminster Assembly* (1904, rpr. Greenville, SC, A Press, 1991).

William Hetherington, *History of the Westminster Assembly of Divines* (1843; rpr. Still Waters Revival Books, 1991).

John H. Leith, *Assembly at Westminster: Reformed Theology in the Making* (Louisville: John Knox Press, 1973).

Robert Letham, *The Westminster Assembly: Reading Its Theology in Historical Context* (Westminster Assembly and the Reformed Faith) (Phillipsburg, NJ: Presbyterian and Reformed Publishing Co., 2009).

Alexander F. Mitchell (w/ C. Matthew McMahon), *The*

Westminster Assembly: Its History and Standards (1883; rpr. Puritan Publications, 2012; also Still Waters Revival Books, 1993).

A. W. Mitchell, *A History of the Westminster Assembly of Divines: Embracing an Account of Its Principal Transactions, and Biographical Sketches of Its Most Conspicuous Members* (Philadelphia, Presbyterian Board of Publication, 1841).

Robert S. Paul, *The Assembly of the Lord* (Edinburgh: T & T Clark, 1985).

James Reid, *Memoirs of the Westminster Divines* (1811; rpr. Edinburgh: Banner of Truth, 1982).

Thomas Smyth, *The History, Character and Results of the Westminster Assembly of Divines* (rpr. 2013).

Benjamin B. Warfield, *The Westminster Assembly and Its Work* (1931; rpr. Great Christian Books, 2015).

COMMEMORATIONS

Francis R. Beattie, *et al.*, eds., *Memorial Volume of the Westminster Assembly, 1647-1897* (Richmond, VA: The Presbyterian Committee of Publication, 1897).

Samuel Carruthers, *The Every Day Work of the Westminster Assembly* (Presbyterian Historical Society of England, 1943).

Carson, John L. and Hall, David W., eds., *To Glorify and Enjoy: A Commemoration of the Westminster Assembly* (Banner of Truth, 1994).

John Murray, "The Importance and Relevance of the Westminster

Confession," in *Collected Writings of John Murray* (Edinburgh: Banner of Truth, 1976), vol. 1.

Francis Patton, *The Genesis of the Westminster Assembly* (Richmond, VA: The Presbyterian Committee of Publication, 1889).

William Henry Roberts, ed., *Addresses at the celebration of the two hundred and fiftieth anniversary of the Westminster Assembly by the General Assembly of the Presbyterian Church in the U.S.A.* (Philadelphia: Presbyterian Board of Publication, 1898).

COMMENTARIES

Kevin Bidwell, ed., *The Westminster Standards for Today* (Evangelical Press Books, 2017).

Thomas Boston, *An Illustration of the Doctrines of the Christian Religion* (1773; rpr. Wheaton, IL: Richard Owen Roberts Publisher, 1980).

John H. Bower, ed., *The Larger Catechism: A Critical Text and Introduction: Principal Documents of the Westminster Assembly* (Grand Rapids, MI: Reformation Heritage Books, 2010).

Gordon H. Clark, *What Do Presbyterians Believe?* (Jefferson, MD: Trinity Foundation, 2001).

David Dickson, *Truth's Victory Over Error: A Commentary on The Westminster Confession of Faith* (Banner of Truth, 2007).

J. Ligon Duncan, ed., *The Westminster Confession into the Twenty-*

First Century [3 vols] (Edinburgh: Christian Focus, 2003-2009).

Sinclair Ferguson, *The Westminster Standards: Analysis of the Westminster Confession of Faith* (online lecture series at: https://www.thegospelcoalition.org/course/the-westminster-standards/#course-introduction-history

John V. Fesko, *The Theology of the Westminster Standards: Historical Context and Theological Insights* (Wheaton, IL: Crossway, 2014).

James Fisher, *Exposition of the Shorter Catechism* (1753; rpr. Reformation Heritage Books, 2014).

John Flavel, *An Exposition of the Assembly's Shorter Catechism*, web posted at: http://www.shortercatechism.com/resources/flavel/wsc_fl_098.html.

John H. Gerstner, Douglas F. Kelly, et al., *A Guide to the Westminster Confession of Faith* (Signal Mountain, TN: Summertown Texts, 1992).

Matthew Henry, *A Scripture Catechism in the Method of the Assembly's*, web posted at: http://www.shortercatechism.com/resources/henry/wsc_he_098.html.

A. A. Hodge, *The Westminster Confession of Faith: A Commentary* (1869; rpr. Banner of Truth, 1991).

Joseph A. Pipa, *The Westminster Confession of Faith Study Book: A Study Guide for Churches* (Christian Focus, 2005).

Thomas Ridgeley, *Commentary on the Larger Catechism* (1731, rpr. Still Waters Revival Books,1993).

Robert Shaw, *The Reformed Faith: An Exposition of the Westminster Confession of Faith* (1845; rpr. Christian Heritage, 2008).

Morton H. Smith, *Harmony of the Westminster Confession and Catechisms* (Greenville Presbyterian Theological Seminary Press, 1997).

Chad van Dixhoorn, *Confessing the Faith: A Reader's Guide to the Westminster Confession of Faith* (Banner of Truth, 2014).

Thomas Vincent, *Shorter Catechism Explained from Scripture* (1674, rpr. Banner of Truth, 1980).

Johannes G. Vos, *The Westminster Larger Catechism: A Commentary,* G. I. Williamson, ed. (Phillipsburg, NJ: Presbyterian and Reformed Publishing Co., 2002).

Thomas Watson, *A Body of Divinity* [Sermons on the Westminster Assembly's Catechism] (1692; rpr. Banner of Truth, 1958).

Thomas Whitecross, *Anecdotes Illustrative of the Assembly* (rpr. as *The Shorter Catechism Illustrated,* Banner of Truth, 1968)

Alexander Whyte, *An Exposition on the Shorter Catechism* (Christian Heritage, 2004).

T. L. Wilkinson, *The Westminster Confession Now: An Exposition of a Reformation Document with a Message for Today in Today's Language* (np, 1992).

G. I. Williamson, *The Westminster Confession of Faith: For Study Classes* (P & R Publishing, 1964).

MONOGRAPHS

Christopher Coldwell, ed., *The Westminster Assembly's Grand Debates*, (Dallas, TX: Naphtali Press, 2014).

Robert L. Dabney, *The Westminster Confession and Creeds* (Dallas, TX, Presbyterian Heritage Publications, 1993).

John R. de Witt, *Jus Divinum: The Westminster Assembly and the Divine Right of Church Government* (Kampen: J. H. Kok, 1969).

David W. Hall, *Windows on Westminster* (Norcross, GA: Great Commission Publications, 1993).

Larry J. Holley, *The Divines of the Westminster Assembly: A Study of Puritanism and Parliament* (Yale University Press, 1979).

Wayne Spear, *Covenanted Uniformity in Religion: The Influence of the Scottish Commissioners upon the Ecclesiology of the Westminster Assembly* (Grand Rapids, MI: Reformation Heritage Books, 2013).

Chad van Dixhoorn, *God's Ambassadors: The Westminster Assembly and the Reformation of the English Pulpit, 1643-1653* (Grand Rapids, MI: Reformation Heritage Books, 2015).

ONLINE RESOURCES

Westminster Assembly Project Website, Secondary Sources: https://www.westminsterassembly.org/secondary-source/.

For translations of the Westminster Standards, see: https://westminsterstandards.org/.

"Presbyterian Standards" by F. R. Beattie:

http://gallery.myff.org/gallery/1252606/Presbyterian+Standards+Francis+Beattie.pdf

"Resources for the Study of the Westminster Confession of Faith and Catechism," compiled by Wayne Sparkman at: http://www.pcahistory.org/HCLibrary/westminster/index.html

Other Books by David W. Hall @ www.amazon.com

The Genevan Reformation and the American Founding
Savior or Servant? Putting Government in Its Place
Election Day Sermons
Welfare Reformed
Questioning Politics
Declaring Independence
Twenty Messages
Election Sermons
God and Caesar
Evangelical Apologetics
Holding Fast to Creation
Did God Create in Six Days
The Genesis Debate
A Heart Promptly Offered
The Legacy of John Calvin
Calvin in the Public Square
Calvin and Commerce
Preaching Like Calvin
Calvin and Culture
Tributes to John Calvin
Theological Guide to Calvin's Institutes
Lux Supra Tenebrae
Post Tenebrae
Lux
Theology Made Practical
Windows on Westminster
The Westminster Assembly: A Guide to Basic Bibliography
To Glorify and Enjoy God
Divine Character
Jus Divinum
Jus Divinum (abridged): The Divine Plan for Church Structure
Practice of Confessional Subscription
Paradigms in Polity
Manual for Officer Training
On Reforming Worship
Practicing Christian Marriage
The Arrogance of the Modern
The Millennium of Jesus Christ
Summer Reading
Ancient Faith: Enduring Belief

Made in the USA
Columbia, SC
18 July 2019